GW00643465

There are books addre
personal or spiritual per:
the fact that it addresses
You will be challenged
others and his ceaseless 1
never think about the issue the same way again.

David Blevin
Sky News

Written with grace, wisdom, and from personal experience, the book will carefully and gently help readers navigate some difficult pastoral issues relating to mental health.

Peter Orr
Lecturer in New Testament, Moore College, Sydney
Author of *Exalted Above the Heavens*

What a superb book. I so benefited from reading it.

John Samuel
Former pastor of Grosvenor Road Baptist Church, Dublin
Pastor, Duke Street Church, Richmond

This book is good! It feels very real – its credibility stems especially from the fact that its author has experienced being in this place himself. And it's well written! A resource pastors can do well to have accessible on their shelves for when it's needed!

Peter Lowman
Former coordinator of the Russian Christian Union movement

This is a book of compassion and courage. 'Compassion' because Paul Ritchie writes with a pastor's heart for Christians struggling with depression and anxiety – and for friends and relatives who walk alongside them. The pages are full of stories and a practical wisdom, rooted in the Bible, that speak into the emotional turmoil and troubling questions that many believers wrestle with (too often on their own).

'Courage' because here is a leader honest enough to tell his own story of mental ill-health and learning to live with it as a disciple of Jesus. You won't find simple answers here, but you will find a real, down-to-earth guide to help you on your way.

Patrick Mitchel
Senior Lecturer in Theology, Irish Bible Institute, Dublin
Author of *The Message of Love*

As a teacher of pastoral care at the Irish Bible Institute it is great to have such an honest and real book about depression and anxiety written in the Irish context by a church leader who has battled with these things and yet through all that has had the desire to live for God and honour Him. It deals with many of the misconceptions and misunderstandings that exist around these issues. The prayers at the end of each chapter that are based on the Psalms are so helpful. The overriding message of this book is that you can know God, the true God, as He has revealed Himself in the Scriptures in whatever you are facing in life, and know His love and care.

Joan Singleton
Lecturer in Pastoral Care, Irish Bible Institute, Dublin, Ireland

Honest, human and heart-felt, every page is borne of Paul's own walk through the darkness. This is not a handbook of plastic solutions, but a companion to walking through the mess more closely with Jesus and in light of His grace. Immensely helpful and moving; essential reading for every believer.

Mark Ellis
Director, Christian Unions Ireland

Is it Unspiritual *to Be* Depressed?

*Loved by God
in the Midst of Pain*

Paul Ritchie

CHRISTIAN
FOCUS

Copyright © Paul Ritchie 2022

paperback ISBN 978-1-5271-0789-2
ebook ISBN 978-1-5271-0863-9

Published in 2022 by
Christian Focus Publications Ltd,
Geanies House, Fearn, Ross-shire,
IV20 1TW, Scotland
www.christianfocus.com

A CIP catalogue record for this book is available
from the British Library.

Cover design by Rubner Durais

Printed and bound by Bell & Bain, Glasgow

Note: Some names have been changed to protect the privacy of those mentioned.

Contents

Foreword

I thought I was there for Paul. It turned out Paul was there for me. It was spring 2007. I had been offered a place to study Applied Theology at the Irish Bible Institute in Dublin and needed a student placement. When we heard that a church situated four miles from our home needed a pastoral assistant, we knew a plan was taking shape. The pastor, who had been ill for a time, was returning. Surely, I was being sent there 'for such a time as this' – a time when I could support him in his ministry to this congregation.

They were a warm and welcoming people but there was something different about this church. At first, it seemed like a disproportionate number of them were suffering with mental illness but that was not the case at all. They had just been given permission to talk about it. By openly talking about his own mental health, their pastor had challenged the stigma. His authenticity was refreshing. Long before it was fashionable to talk about these things in the church, Paul had created a safe space in which people could take off their Sunday mask and speak openly about mental illness.

In this short book, he shares his own story with courage and tackles the question of mental health and Christian faith. There is a plethora of self-help books on the shelves for those dealing with mental illness. This is not another one. While Paul draws on the experience of well-known figures in church history who have also struggled in this area, he ultimately points his readers towards the God-inspired pages of the Bible – unshakeable truths to hold onto, light in the deepest darkness. Read it, let it take root in your heart and you will find refreshment for your soul.

This book is for those who struggle and for those who journey with them. I am in the latter category. For most of her adult life, my wife had suffered in silence. Her mental health reached breaking point while I was serving alongside Paul. We had indeed been sent there 'for such a time as this' – a time when we needed to be among people who would both understand and support us. I thought I was there for Paul. It turned out Paul was there for me. I thank God for him and for the insights contained in these pages.

David Blevins
Sky News

INTRODUCTION

'How long must I wrestle with my thoughts?'
(Psalm 13:2)

I was thirteen. I had prayed the 'sinner's prayer' asking Jesus into my life at a Scripture Union camp a couple of years before, although I am not sure how real my faith actually was. As a family, we were on a camping holiday in France. It was a humid night and a thunderstorm was brewing. I couldn't get to sleep. A thought came into my head: What would happen if I said a satanic prayer? I am not too sure where this idea came from. I had read the book *From Witchcraft to Christ*. Perhaps that was the root of my thinking. The author of that book had done some 'miraculous' things when she had been a witch.

I didn't want to give in to the temptation. I resisted and resisted, hoping to fall asleep, but the humidity kept me awake and my curiosity was immense. Eventually I did give in. I don't remember what I prayed, and I don't like to think about it. When nothing magical happened,

I acknowledged to God that I had been a fool. However, later that evening the storm erupted. As the lightning flashed and thunder crashed, I feared that God was expressing His rage at what I had done. I was very worried. The next morning, I asked my mother if God forgives everything we confess, and she promised me that He did. I didn't think of that incident for years, but it later came back to haunt me.

In my very late teens and early twenties, I came across verses about the unforgiveable sin and the warning passages in the book of Hebrews about falling away. These warning passages became an obsession for me. I wondered how my dabbling with satanism as a thirteen-year-old could have been anything other than an irrevocable falling away. I thought about this all the time. I consulted Bible commentary after commentary looking for reassurance but I could not shake off the fear. Most of the time I functioned fairly normally. I came across as a happy person, but there was always insecurity and at times my anxieties would flair up. I went through at least one episode of depression where my appetite disappeared, my mood was desperately low, and I would wake early in the morning unable to sleep again. These fears lasted all through my twenties. The nature of my anxieties changed as I approached thirty. As well as my fear of being beyond God's forgiveness, I began to struggle to keep certain thoughts out of my mind. These thoughts could be very dark and disturbing. I had little rituals to help deal with them, like holding my thumb underneath my ring finger, as a physical gesture to say, 'I don't like this thought that I fear I am going to give in to.' I would also mumble under my breath. I remember going to a church service and the friend sitting behind me commenting on how fidgety I was. I was wrestling so hard not to give in to these dark thoughts that it even showed in my bodily posture. It was embarrassing to try and explain to anyone what was going on in my mind. Even now I can see how odd this must have seemed.

A few years after these intrusive thoughts had begun to trouble me we were on a short holiday in Tipperary. My parents, my sister's family and my brother's family were there too. One night, the adults were sitting around the table after the meal when my mother mentioned that my dad's mother had struggled with debilitating mental illness and had spent many years in care. It wasn't that this had been kept a secret, but I never remember it being mentioned before. A light went on in my head: Could it be that these intrusive thoughts that I battle to keep out of my head aren't simply a case of me being silly? Maybe I have inherited a predisposition to anxiety. Maybe there is some medical root to what I am suffering.

I didn't go to the doctor straight away but, at a time when my thoughts were unmanageable, I did eventually go. In God's kindness, there happened to be a couple of general practitioners and a psychiatrist in the church I was pastoring. Rosie, who could see that I was struggling, gave me some tablets and arranged for Stephen, the psychiatrist, to visit me at home.

That night Stephen turned up at our house. He heard what I was saying about my disturbing thoughts and the little rituals I had to deal with them, and he immediately diagnosed the problem. He described my thoughts as being ridiculous, resistant, repetitive and repulsive to me. That is exactly what they were. He said that I was suffering from obsessive-compulsive disorder (OCD). I would never have guessed that because, like many people, I thought OCD was always about cleaning things whereas I am an untidy person. Stephen told me to take two months off work, prescribed some medication and recommended that I take a course in cognitive behaviour therapy (CBT).

My OCD became much more manageable over the following years. I know that some of my friends have had difficulty connecting with their cognitive behaviour therapist, but mine was brilliant. I felt completely free to talk to her, even about things that were deeply embarrassing. CBT taught me how to understand my thoughts, and I kept on taking my tablets every day. Things were good.

Coming up to Christmas 2017 a number of changes in my life increased my stress levels. My wife, Caroline, had started part-time work outside of the home and I was trying to figure out the balance between family responsibilities and work. There were also some changes taking place in my work with the church. Then there was the fact that I had fallen behind in taking my tablets because I had not got around to renewing my prescription.

One Friday evening I was with my wife and kids, and I started to become very anxious. Old fears of being unforgivable re-emerged. I quietly slipped upstairs and got into bed, where I began to shake with nerves. I was having some sort of breakdown. For a week I was in a bad way and stayed in bed. I was prescribed a lot of sedatives, and these helped. After a couple of weeks, I was feeling better again. It seemed as if the episode was over. Then one day a darkness came over me. For the next number of weeks, I was deeply depressed and anxious. My thoughts were very troubled. I was racked with doubt. I not only wondered if God loved me, I wondered if He even existed. I had little appetite and lost a good amount of weight. I could get to sleep, but I would wake early in the morning with my feet dripping with sweat. (I am not sure why it was my feet that sweated so much!) The Irish rugby team were on their way to winning the Grand Slam, yet I only watched the matches to be with my son and act as if things were normal. In truth I couldn't enjoy anything. This depression was unlike any other episode that I had had and I was scared that it would never lift. I feared that life would always be this way. Thankfully, it did lift, although I persisted with a mildly low mood for a long time afterwards.

Things are good now, though I sometimes still wake up in a low mood. I suspect there may well be further instances of depression and anxiety in the future. Yet I am sure I will get through them, as I got through on previous occasions. In some ways, getting through the last episode of depression and anxiety has strengthened me.

I WANT YOU TO KNOW THAT GOD IS WITH YOU

In this book, I want to draw on my own experiences and thoughts on issues related to depression and anxiety. I am coming from an evangelical Christian perspective and I want to show you how the good news about Jesus is good news for your mental health. I want to do something to take away the stigma and misunderstanding that surrounds mental illness, particularly in church circles. There is also a chapter for those of you seeking to help people in your church or family who struggle with depression and anxiety.

My hope is that, as you read this short book, your confidence in the kindness of God will grow, and you will experience the truth that 'the Lord is close to the brokenhearted and saves those who are crushed in spirit' (Ps. 34:18).

Let's pray to the Father:

'How long, Lord? Will You forget me forever? How long will You hide Your face from me? How long must I wrestle with my thoughts and day after day have sorrow in my heart?' (Ps. 13:1-2). Father, my thoughts trouble me and I feel no joy. Help me, please. I am anxious and losing hope. Please show me the way out of this dark tunnel, for I can't see any light. You are my rock and my refuge to whom I can always go for comfort and rest. (Ps. 71:3). Amen.

1

WHY DO PEOPLE STRUGGLE WITH DEPRESSION AND ANXIETY?

'Everything is needful that He sends; nothing can be needful that He withholds.'[1]
(John Newton)

If I was to think of why I struggle with depression and anxiety, I might come up with a number of factors and causes. There were my terrible fears that I was beyond the reach of God. There was also the possibility of a hereditary factor – after all, my grandmother suffered with depression and anxiety. Perhaps a traumatic incident of bullying in my first year as a boarder in school contributed to my sense of anxiety. What about the loneliness that I experienced when I finished as a boarder and later when I began to work in churches? At the time of my breakdown, I was under pressure balancing work and home life. All these factors and more may have contributed to my mental health problems.

---

1. Quoted in Timothy Keller, *Walking with God through Pain and Suffering* (London: Hodder and Stoughton Limited, 2013), p. 266.

I want to suggest that all these factors have a shared root: the fact that we live in a fallen world! 'The Fall' describes how the first humans, Adam and Eve, rebelled against God and, as a result of God's subsequent judgement, we now live subject to sickness, sin, decay, hostility, loneliness and death. This judgement on human rebellion is called 'the Curse'.

WHAT ARE DEPRESSION AND ANXIETY?

Before I show you how the Fall and the Curse cause depression and anxiety, I need to explain what depression and anxiety actually are. After all, we all go through days when we are less positive about life than others, and every day there are things that we can feel worried about. Depression involves a persisting low mood. Depressed people feel an almost constant state of sadness. The depressed person no longer enjoys activities that used to bring them pleasure. You may not be suicidal, but you don't really want to be living. Your thoughts are generally gloomy, and you may be experiencing changes in appetite and sleep patterns. If this goes on for more than two weeks, it's generally considered a depressive episode.

The issues can be similar with anxiety. Changes in sleeping and eating patterns may be evident. Your life is dominated by worries and you might struggle with disturbing thoughts. Your fears may seem unrealistic to others. Your worry is out of proportion. You are pessimistic about the future. You tend to overestimate the sense of threat and underestimate your ability to cope. Your anxiety could be a temporary reaction to external stresses, or you could be struggling with an anxiety disorder. Anxiety and depression are often interrelated.

HOW ARE DEPRESSION AND ANXIETY CAUSED BY THE FALL AND THE CURSE?

God had told Adam that if he and Eve rebelled against His loving rule, they would die. Adam and Eve did rebel. They no longer wanted to live under God's rule, and death entered the human experience. We now have mortal bodies that are subject to sickness and decay. Every part of our body is affected, including our brains. Our brains no longer function perfectly. Mental illness, like physical illness, is a part of the common lot of humankind.

Besides affecting our bodies and minds, the Fall and the Curse also affect us spiritually. Humankind is now born with what is called a sinful nature. This means that we have a natural tendency towards self-centredness and a natural hostility towards living under the loving rule of God. We also have a hostility towards other people, and so we don't live in harmony. This is seen in the life of Cain and Abel, the sons of Adam and Eve. Cain was jealous of Abel and murdered him. A big factor in our depression and anxiety is the hurt that other people do to us. They may not murder us, but they can be less than loving. Many victims of abuse struggle with mental health issues. Difficult marriages or family relations can be a huge source of pressure. People carry the wounds caused by an unloving parent, a harsh teacher or a school bully. I have a friend whose mother used to wake her in the middle of the night in order to tell her that she was worthless. This contributed to mental health problems later in her life. Sometimes adverse reactions to the hurt caused by others don't surface until years after the events that wounded so deeply. King David knew what it felt like to feel worn down by other people. He wrote: 'My eyes grow weak with sorrow; they fail because of all my foes' (Ps. 6:7).

We are not simply the victims of other people's sinful nature. We are the victims of our own sinful hearts and foolish choices. For example, we struggle with anger when we don't get our way. Uncontrolled anger has been shown to set a person up for stress, depression, anxiety and even heart attacks. 'A heart at peace gives life to the body, but envy rots the bones' (Prov. 14:30). Of course, not all anger is condemned in the Bible; there is something called righteous anger. We should be angered when we witness cruelty and injustice. Most of my anger is anything but righteous. My anger is generally selfish and ignoble. We can't deal with anger on our own, so God has given His people the Holy Spirit who produces His fruit in our lives, which includes self-control (Gal. 5:23).

Bitterness also eats us up emotionally, like an acid destroying its own container. If you hold grudges against people, it will make you miserable. This is one of the beautiful things about the Christian gospel. God sent His Son to die for wicked people, so that our sins can be forgiven. As forgiven people, we are to forgive others. Part of my friend Andy's depression has roots in the hurt caused by a school bully. His psychiatrist had him fill out a forgiveness worksheet. I asked him, 'Do you think you could have forgiven him without your faith?' 'No', he immediately replied. 'I wouldn't have wanted to forgive him.' He was honest enough to admit that some of the bitterness still lives with him, but he knows that he has been called to let it go. This takes time. I am not saying that only Christians practise forgiveness but the good news about Jesus is the motivation to practise it and we are promised God's power to enable us in this most difficult of tasks. Letting go of bitterness is very good for your mental health. If you are bitter, you will hurt no one more than yourself.

God may cause us to feel sorrow and restlessness when we stray from Him as a means to bring us home. When King David committed adultery and then arranged matters so that the woman's husband was killed, he refused to face up to what he had done. God loved him too much to let him go on like this. David says of that time of denial, 'When I kept silent, my bones wasted away through my groaning all day long … Then I acknowledged my sin to you and did not cover up my iniquity. I said, "I will confess my transgressions to the Lord." And you forgave the guilt of my sin' (Ps. 32:3-5). When I pray with people for physical and emotional healing, I allow for a time of silence where we can confess our sin. However, being depressed and anxious does not necessarily mean we have committed some particular sin to cause it. If God is using this pain to call you back to Himself, He will make that clear. Never assume that your depression and anxiety is caused by some unconfessed sin. Never accuse someone who is depressed or anxious of having done something wrong to bring about their pain. There are many other reasons why people struggle with anxiety and depression.

One of the results of the Fall and the Curse is that work is difficult. You may be over-worked and under-rested. In the Old Testament, when the prophet Elijah became weary and despondent, God saw that what he needed was food and rest (1 Kings 19:4-5, 7). I have noticed that many depressed and anxious people have an exaggerated sense of responsibility that can drive them mercilessly. They blame themselves for everything that goes wrong and feel the need for everything to go right. God calls us to rest and trust that He is in control.

The Fall and Curse means that we all will die. The loss of those we love can be very difficult. Grief is a normal and healthy reaction to loss. However, it can become debilitating. I knew a man who died not long after his wife. I couldn't help wondering if he actually died of a broken heart. Similarly, I remember an elderly woman who experienced debilitating mental health after the death of her brother. God wants us to lean on Him in our grief, as He promises to be with us while we travel through the valley of death (Ps. 23:4).

Then there is the problem of our own death. Most of us find ageing difficult. Fear of dying can begin long before old age. The hard truth is that we all will die. That thought can be very disturbing. However, the good news of the death and resurrection of Jesus gives us hope in the face of our own mortality. Jesus has defeated death. He now offers people eternal life. Though we have to live in this fallen world now, when we die, our suffering and pain will be over. Jesus wants to free us from the fear of death (Heb. 2:15). In God's new heaven and new earth there will be no more Curse and no more tears (Rev. 21:4, 22:3).

Martin Luther, the sixteenth-century reformer, struggled with bouts of deep anxiety and depression. He had a sensitive temperament, a difficult relationship with his father and he faced fierce opposition. At one stage he felt responsible for the fact that some of his followers were dying for their faith, while he lay safely in his bed. However, while outward events affected him, the very nature of 'the dark night of the soul' is that it sometimes appears without any obvious cause. There may seem to be little explanation as to why we can cope with some pressures well at one time, and then at other times we fall apart. My wife, Caroline, often asks what has changed in my life when my anxieties begin to get out of control. While sometimes I can see certain factors at work, other times I can think of nothing that has caused the deterioration.

Conclusion

If you are struggling with depression and anxiety, can you pinpoint some of the factors that may contribute to it? How was your life when you were growing up? What was your relationship with your parents or guardians like? Are there other members of your family who struggle with their mental health? Could you have a hereditary predisposition? Is life very stressful for you?

Most likely there will be many factors contributing to your depression and anxiety, some of which you have not even considered. Since there can be a number of factors, you should seek a number of 'helps' in dealing with it. You may need some combination of rest, medical help, counselling and spiritual guidance. While there are many factors at work causing your struggles with mental health, all these are rooted in the fact that we live in a fallen world that is subject to sin, decay, isolation and death. I heard one preacher say that since he had become a Christian he had not suffered so much as a cold. He obviously had a good immune system, but terrible theology. To deny that the Christian suffers from physical and mental brokenness in this life is to misunderstand the nature of living in a fallen world.

Thankfully the Fall and the Curse were not the last Word of God for humankind. The ultimate hope for the depressed Christian is that we are heading to a future where there will be no more tears. However, our hope does not simply lie beyond this life. Even now, we have a Heavenly Father who will never forsake us even though we have often turned our backs on Him. The Fall and Curse may lie behind all our depression and anxiety, but so does God. After all, He rules over everything that takes place in this fallen world. Enemies may wound us, but God could shut their mouths. Circumstances may hurt us, but God is in control of all things. Similarly, our brain chemistry is not beyond His ordering.

During my time of deep depression, Caroline and I were helped by a quote from the slave-trader turned hymn-writer, John Newton. Newton wrote, 'Everything is needful that He sends; nothing can be needful that He withholds.'

God being in control may leave us with some painful and difficult questions: 'Why would God allow me to pass through this pain? Why can't I feel His presence? Why does my faith lack assurance? Will this anxiety go away?' At times we are baffled. But it is better to be in the hands of the God beyond our understanding who is in control of all things, than living at the mercy of blind chaos – especially when that God has invited me to call Him Father.

Let's pray to the Father:

Father, You see the anguish of my soul and my affliction. Turn Your ear to me and come quickly to my rescue. Be merciful to me for I am in distress. My eyes are weak with sorrow, my body with grief. My life is consumed with anguish, and my years with groaning. Help me to trust in You. Bring me to the place where I can confidently say, 'You are my God.' Let Your face shine on me and lift my darkness. Be my hope and make my heart strong. Amen.

(Adapted from Psalm 31)

2

IS CHRISTIANITY GOOD FOR OUR MENTAL HEALTH?

*'Just think what it would be like to be certain that
the God of this universe loved you. That alone would
probably change the contours of depression.'[1]*
(Ed Welch)

A friend gave me a booklet which stated that spirituality
is good for your mental health. It gives people a feeling
of being part of something bigger than themselves and
it is helpful to be a part of a faith community. Professor
Andrew Simms, former President of the Royal College
of Psychiatrists, comments that, 'The advantageous
effect of religious belief and spirituality on mental
and physical health is one of the best-kept secrets in
psychiatry and medicine generally.'[2]

---

1. Edward T. Welch, *Depression: Looking up from the Stubborn Darkness* (Greensboro, North Carolina: New Growth Press, 2011), p. 113.

2. Quoted in John C. Lennox, *Gunning for God: Why the New Atheists are Missing the Target* (Oxford: Lion Hudson, 2011), p. 59.

I think Christianity has a unique benefit over other religions. While other beliefs speak of living for the acceptance of a god or gods, the Christian gospel of grace tells us that God accepts people on the basis of free, undeserved, unearned and unmerited favour. The Christian gospel doesn't say 'change your life and God will accept you', but rather 'embrace God's acceptance and that will change your life'.

It's also worth comparing the Christian gospel of grace with society's teaching on self-esteem. Popular culture tells us to seek our value by searching for 'the hero inside ourselves'. The problem is that when I examine my life, I see many things that make me feel ashamed. Instead of a hero, I often see a villain. I have to admit that I am selfish and self-centred. I don't say this because I have low self-esteem. I say this because it is true. If my emotional well-being is built on the existence of an inner hero, then I am going to struggle within. Trying to convince yourself that you are really good at heart is a poor foundation on which to build your mental health.

THE CHRISTIAN MESSAGE SAYS THAT GOD TREATS US WITH A LOVE WE DO NOT DESERVE

The gospel of grace says that I am a flawed and rebellious person who is loved by a kind and forgiving Creator. This Creator, making us in His image, has given each of us intrinsic worth. This God cares for us so much that He sent His Son to die for our past, present and future guilt. This God treats me not as my sins deserve, but according to His loving-kindness. This love is seen most clearly as you contemplate the cross of Jesus

(1 John 3:16). Think of the Father who loved you so much that He gave His one and only Son so that you would not perish but have eternal life (John 3:16). Think of the Son of God who loved you and gave Himself for you (Gal. 2:20). If you have taken hold of this gospel of grace, then you need to be reminding yourself of this good news every day, especially when God seems distant or absent. The reality of God's love for you does not depend on your emotional ability to feel it.

However, I need to be balanced here. When people grow up with a distortion of Christianity, it can result in emotional and mental suffering. One friend told me that he grew up with a mother who seemed to want to frighten him into following Jesus. Another friend carries deep wounds from the way her church treated her as a teenager. A couple of boys came home from a mission meeting and asked their mother, 'Why was the speaker so angry with us?' That mission speaker didn't convey to those young minds a gentle image of God. When churches and homes define Christianity simply in terms of 'dos and don'ts' and when they are expert at seeing the flaws in others, they raise people with hyper-sensitive consciences and emotional insecurity. The gospel of grace should be good news for our mental health, but when God is thought of as vindictive and unkind, then faith can actually hurt us.

To be a Christian is to be a subject of God's delight

When you are depressed and anxious, you are vulnerable to believing lies about God. In our darkest moments, nothing matters more than knowing that God loves us, and yet it can be so hard to feel His love then. When we forget, or are unable to grasp, that God is a loving Father who always seeks the good of His children, we will struggle emotionally. Martin Luther struggled with depression and anxiety even after he had come to understand the gracious nature of the good news about Jesus. He said that his depression always centred on two questions: 'Is God good?' and 'Is God good to me?' Think of how wonderful it would be to be sure that the God of this universe is kind and that He loves you with a love beyond measure.

To be in a living relationship with Jesus is to be a subject of God's delight. It is a wonderful thing to realise that our God is pleased even by our imperfect efforts to serve Him. He sees everything that we do for Him, even when no one else notices. Jesus breathes His grace over our sin-stained half-baked efforts to honour God and makes them perfect in the eyes of our Heavenly Father. God delights in all that we do for Him in love. While Jesus does call us to a challenging life, He is also kind and understanding. He tells us to take up our cross (Luke 9:23), but also says that He is 'gentle and humble in heart', and in Him you 'will find rest for your souls' (Matt. 11:29). Jesus is aware of our vulnerabilities and will not push us beyond what we can bear. Jesus will not break a bruised reed or snuff out a smouldering wick (Isa. 42:3 and Matt. 12:20). He is not like the parent who may have driven you to always work more and play harder.

God doesn't just delight in what we do. He delights that we belong to Him, even when our walk with Him isn't going so well. I asked a depressed and anxious friend if he believed that God rejoiced over him with singing (Zeph. 3:17). He said, 'It seems too good to be true.' But it is true! Believe it and be glad! It is really important to grow in your awareness of the goodness of God.

You are an object of God's delight but you are also the focus of Satan's hatred. Satan is a factor in depression and anxiety. Not in a wacky sense, but in the fact that he will remind you of past guilt, tempt you towards bitterness and seek to implant in you doubts about the goodness of God (Gen. 3:1-5). When the devil reminds you of your past and present sin, remind yourself that Jesus frees you from all condemnation (Rom. 8:1). In the book of Revelation, Christians triumph over the accusations of the evil one through the blood of the Lamb and the word of their testimony (Rev. 12:11). In other words, they remember that Jesus died for all their guilt and that they are accepted by grace.

TRY TO HOLD ON TO YOUR CONFIDENCE IN THE GOODNESS OF GOD

Near the end of my last episode of deep depression I struggled with my confidence in the goodness of God. In particular I felt upset about the theme of God's judgement. I obsessively thought, 'How can a God of love send people to hell?' I was miserable thinking of people being condemned without a living relationship with Jesus. The gospel didn't seem like good news to me. I still often struggle with this hard truth.

It is actually healthy that we should feel sorrow about those who reject Christ's offer of new life and will face God's judgement. Jesus felt this same sorrow as He looked over the rebellious city of Jerusalem and cried, 'Jerusalem, Jerusalem, you who kill the prophets and stone those sent to you, how often I have longed to gather your children together, as a hen gathers her chicks under her wings, and you were not willing' (Matt. 23:37). When a rich young ruler approached Him, Jesus looked at him and loved him (Mark 10:21). Surely Jesus' heart broke as He saw that man walk away refusing to put God first in his life and to experience all that God had for him.

The apostle Paul felt this sorrow. He speaks of the unceasing anguish in his heart for his people, the Jews (Rom. 9:2-3). None of us love people as much as Christ loves them. 'As surely as I live, declares the Sovereign Lord, I take no pleasure in the death of the wicked, but would rather that they turn from their ways and live … Turn from your evil ways!' (Ezek. 33:11). Our sorrow over those who refuse to be drawn to Jesus should motivate us to pray for them and to ask God for opportunities to speak about Him. Jesus' bewilderment was not that people would be judged because of their wickedness, but that they refused the forgiveness and life He longed for them to receive. Hell stands as a testimony to the stubbornness of the human heart in the face of amazing grace.

Perhaps God's judgement is not the issue that causes you to question the goodness of God. It may be other hard truths. As our society moves further and further from its Christian roots, we can feel the tension between what those around us believe is good and true, and what the Bible says is good and true. This may be hardest for younger Christians. They are constantly being told that such things as Christian sexual ethics are outdated, narrow-minded and even bigoted. These Bible teachings can be hard to accept. The willingness of Christian young people to hold these teachings may leave them feeling isolated from their friends and their culture. This can be a source of great pain and stress. It may be even more painful if they themselves are working through issues regarding their own sexuality. We need to listen to and support young people in the church when it is tough to be a Christian at school, college or work. We need to help them see that God is loving towards all He has made. (Ps. 145:9). Even though His ways may be a mystery to us, He can be trusted to know what is best for human flourishing.

THERE ARE TIMES TO PUT YOUR DOUBTS ON THE SHELF
John rang me up one day because he was having a bad day with his depression. He mentioned a text from the Bible that he couldn't get his head around. These verses seemed to present God in a negative light. I suggested that now was not a good time for him to wrestle with this passage. There are times when it is okay to put your doubts about the goodness of God or your worries about your relationship with Him on the shelf. I am not saying that we sweep them under the carpet – that would be to live in denial. To put an issue on the shelf is simply saying, 'I can't get my head around this issue right now, but I need to stop continually thinking about it. I will put it on the shelf for a while and come back to it at a more appropriate time.' This is not always easy as our thoughts may be obsessive. Depression and anxiety can have a significant influence on how we feel about

God, which is very distressing for the Christian. But times of mental crisis are not good times for wrestling with the most faith-stretching issues. Try to keep your faith simple when your brain is exhausted.

THANK GOD FOR ALL THAT HE HAS DONE, ESPECIALLY THAT HE HAS FORGIVEN YOU

One of the most unhelpful things that you can do is to ruminate over feelings of guilt and memories of sinful failure. The Christian knows that God is their gracious Heavenly Father. God is slow to anger and abounding in love (Ps. 103:8). He does not treat us as our sins deserve, but according to His loving-kindness (Ps. 103:10). He delights to forgive and there is never any condemnation for those who are in Christ (Rom. 8:1). He is the God who freely pardons (Isa. 55:7). God wants you to rejoice in His forgiveness (Ps. 32:1-2). It does not honour God to keep on reminding yourself of past failures. After all, if He has chosen to remember our sins no more (Heb. 8:12), who are we to remind Him of them? He wants us to rejoice in His grace and be glad.

I asked one lady what she felt contributed to the nervous breakdown she experienced. She explained that at her stage in life, in her early eighties, she had started looking back and thinking about what she could have done better. She says that now she won't allow herself to think like this. 'God has forgiven all these things and doesn't want me to dwell on them.' An attitude of thanksgiving has been a great help to her. She spends time thinking of things to thank God for. In *Wrestling with my Thoughts,* Sharon Hastings writes movingly of her battle with severe mental illness. At the end of her memoir she has still not been healed. Mental health issues are something that she will probably endure for the rest of her life. But she can see that God has not deserted her, even in the darkest of days.

Thanksgiving is good for your mental health. It gives a sense of well-being and increases positivity. It helps counteract negative thoughts like envy, resentment and bitterness and can help us become more loving and empathetic. The Bible is filled with thanksgiving. In the book of Psalms, we are told to thank God because 'he is good' and 'his love endures forever' (Ps. 106:1), for answered prayer and salvation (Ps. 118:21), for His teachings (Ps. 119:62) and simply for who God is (Ps. 106:47). We see Jesus giving thanks for the provision of food. The apostle Paul regularly told the early Christians how thankful to God he was for them and instructed us to present our requests with thanksgiving (Phil. 4:6). When our prayers lack thanksgiving we cut ourselves off from a source of God-given joy.

CONCLUSION: WE HAVE REASON FOR JOY AND HOPE

Is Christianity good for our mental health? It should be. But if we are presented with a harsh view of God, the good news can feel like bad news. One of the most important things for any struggling Christian is to grow in their confidence of the goodness of God.

June had a struggle with depression in her early twenties. She carried a lot of anxiety about her faith. 'It did not feel at times that Christianity was the gospel or good news to me – it was something I had to believe or else I had a perilous end and it seemed to be full of endless rules and regulations that I didn't feel quite up to.' After she was married and living in London she got involved in a kind and gracious church. There was the 'recognition that we are all seeking and walking and stumbling and getting up again. I started to learn that God is a loving and gracious Father; no matter how far I stray or wander, He brings me back onto His path. What Jesus did through the cross became real to me and I began to delight to read the gospels to hear Jesus leaping off the pages. I realised that I had learned a lot of doctrine growing up, but I am not really sure that I had developed a close friendship with Jesus.'

We all live in a fallen world, surrounded by imperfect people, in a decaying body that has an inbuilt tendency towards selfishness. The Christian gospel brings us the good news that we are loved by the God we have rejected and offended. He loves us so much that He gave His Son to die a death that satisfied His justice, so that whoever believes in Him should not suffer condemnation but be accepted as a dearly loved child. This doesn't mean that the Christian gets taken out of this fallen world. We still have bodies that decay, get sick and die. There still are many reasons for tears. But the good news about the death and resurrection of Jesus means that we have reason for joy and peace.

Let's pray to the Father:

Lord, bless You. Thank You for all that You have done for me. Thank You that You forgive everything I have done. You lift me out of the darkness. You love me with an unfailing love. You are merciful and gracious; slow to anger and abounding in love. Your love for me is higher than the heavens are from the earth. You have removed my sins as far as the east is from the west. You are more compassionate than the best of parents. You know all my weaknesses. While my life on earth is short and sometimes painful, Your love is steadfast and sure. Though someday I will be gone and forgotten, Your love for me will never end. Bless You, Lord. Amen.

(Adapted from Psalm 103).

3

Is it unspiritual to be depressed and anxious?

*'I guess joy is not simply an emotion. And so, someone
with depression can still (though it would be harder)
rejoice – have confidence in the Lord.'*
(Peter Orr)

The preacher got up and looked at the congregation. 'Too
many of you are taking tablets for your depression. Where
is your joy in the Lord? If you were depending on God,
you wouldn't need your medication.' I wish I could say that
these words are fictional, but they are not. I have heard of
depressed and anxious people having guilt added to their
distress by such words from the pulpit. In this chapter I want
to show you that these words are not fair. The good news of
grace does offer us joy and peace, but Christians may still
struggle with their mental health as we live in a fallen world.

THE WONDERFUL DEPRESSED AND ANXIOUS CHRISTIANS WHO HAVE GONE BEFORE US

Many godly Christians have struggled through times
of immense sorrow and worry. The great nineteenth-

century Baptist preacher, Charles Spurgeon, struggled with depression throughout his life. What seems to have ignited this was a specific tragedy. Spurgeon was preaching to a huge congregation of over twelve thousand people at the Surrey Music Hall in London when someone yelled 'Fire!' It was a prank. In the chaos that ensued seven people were killed, and Spurgeon was inconsolable. Other factors contributed to his depression, including his struggles with gout and his concern for those he pastored. Like many pastors he was good at caring for his flock's needs but sometimes negligent of his own. He knew times when he would have been very happy to die.

Spurgeon said that there are dungeons beneath the Castle of Despair and that he had often been in them. Of a major bout of despondency that occurred when he was twenty-four, he wrote, 'My Spirits were sunken so low that I could weep by the hour like a child, and yet I knew not what I wept for.'[1]

In the book of Psalms, we often hear the psalmists crying out to God in emotional pain. 'My soul is in deep anguish. How long, LORD, how long?' (Ps. 6:3). 'All night long I flood my bed with weeping and drench my couch with tears' (Ps. 6:6). 'Why, LORD, do you stand far off? Why do you hide yourself in times of trouble?' (Ps. 10:1). Many of the Psalms can be classified as psalms of individual lament, which means that they are the divinely inspired words of an individual who is pouring out their pain to God. These Psalms are given to us by

---

1. Quoted in Terry Powell, 'The "Depression-Prone" Pastor', *Broken Believers* (http://brokenbelievers.com/2017/11/24/recurring-depression-and-faitgful-minsitry/), accessed 19/03/2021.

God in part to help us express our pain and sorrow. These Psalms were quoted in prayers by Jesus who could identify with their pain!

Jesus was a man of sorrows, familiar with grief (Isa. 53:3). In Gethsemane Jesus was deeply sorrowful and troubled (Matt. 26:36-46). From the cross He quoted the Psalms, crying out, 'My God, my God, why have you forsaken me?' (Ps. 22:1 and Mark 15:34). The writer to the Hebrews tells us that Jesus 'offered up prayers and petitions with fervent cries and tears' (Heb. 5:7). Spurgeon wrote, 'No sin is necessarily connected with sorrow of the heart, for Jesus Christ our Lord once said, "My soul is exceedingly sorrowful, even to death." There was no sin in Him, and consequently none in His depression.'[2]

However, be careful! In your depression, do not sin! Depression does present us with particular temptations, such as self-pity. Some people try to find comfort in things like overeating, overworking, abusing alcohol or other substances. While it can be difficult to remain patient with people as you struggle with your own feelings and thoughts, your depression and anxiety does not justify treating people around you in a less than loving way.

AM I LESS SPIRITUAL WHEN I AM DEPRESSED? AFTER ALL, THE FRUIT OF THE SPIRIT INCLUDES JOY

I put this question to a friend, who is a lecturer in a leading evangelical theological college. He replied, 'I

---

2. Charles Spurgeon, 'The Valley of the Shadow of Death', *Metropolitan Tabernacle Pulpit,* Volume 27, (The Spurgeon Centre.Org), accessed 19/03/2021.

guess joy is not simply an emotion. And so, someone with depression can still (though it would be harder) rejoice – have confidence in the Lord.' He then said that Psalm 31:7-9 might be worth looking at. That psalm reads, 'I will be glad and rejoice in your love, for you saw my affliction and knew the anguish of my soul … Be merciful to me, LORD, for I am in distress; my eyes grow weak with sorrow, my soul and body with grief.' Here we can see that anguish of soul and trust in God can go hand in hand, and the psalmist seems to be experiencing both at the same time. This is surely an example of being sorrowful, yet always rejoicing (2 Cor. 6:10).

Joan Singleton lectures in pastoral care in the Irish Bible Institute. She had wondered if her depression inhibited her witness as a Christian until she realised that hanging on to God, even though her life was filled with pain, brought glory to God.

BUT WHAT ABOUT ANXIETY; ISN'T IT WRONG TO WORRY?
I do not dispute that worry can be a sin, but anxiety can have many roots, some of which are not sinful. I actually see a parallel between anxiety and doubt, which itself can be a form of worry.

On certain occasions, Jesus rebuked the disciples for their doubt, because it revealed a stubborn refusal to accept the truth. When the other disciples told Thomas that they had seen the risen Lord, he refused to believe, even though Jesus had spoken of His resurrection and his friends had no reason to lie to him. He even seems to still be doubting when Jesus comes and stands in front of him, so our Lord says, 'Stop doubting and believe' (John 20:27). Yet in the letter of Jude we read that we are to 'be merciful to those who doubt' (Jude 22). Jude was referring to those who doubted, not because they stubbornly refused to believe, but because false teachers had infiltrated the church and upset their faith. There is doubt that deserves a rebuke, and doubt that needs gentle pastoral support. Similarly, there is anxiety that should be challenged, and anxiety that needs gentle pastoral care.

Sinful anxiety is rooted in a failure to trust God or in the fact that we have made peripheral things too important in our lives. If our anxiety is rooted in the fact that our neighbour is doing better than us, that people aren't making us feel important or that we mightn't achieve every goal that we are aiming for, then surely Jesus would tell us to stop worrying and find our identity and security in Him. However, not all anxiety is wrong. The apostle Paul experienced an anxiety related to his love for some of the churches he cared for (2 Cor. 11:28). In many of the Psalms, God gives us words to express our anxiety, often with the purpose of working through our anxiety to a place of hope. Sometimes people have reached a stage of exhaustion that means that they are struggling to think straight. Until they rest, they may find it impossible to hold onto the promises of God. When our anxiety has roots in a distorted view of God, we need to be gently instructed in the truth of His gentleness and grace. We are told to cast our anxieties on the Lord, because He cares for us (1 Pet. 5:7), but some people need help to come to understand that He really does care for them. The person with an anxiety disorder may not even be fully aware why they are so anxious. Their worries may have as much to do with imbalances in brain chemistry as the actual issues they are focusing on. It would simply be too harsh to tell them to stop worrying.

IS IT OKAY TO TAKE ANTIDEPRESSANTS?

John Piper was asked the following question: 'What do you think of Christians taking antidepressants? I have been on them and have been accused of not relying on God'.[3] In his answer, Piper takes a drink from a bottle of water and then asks, 'Was that sip a failure to rely on God?' Could God not keep his throat miraculously moist? Piper's point is that God has given certain means to provide for our physical well-being and these are to be taken with thanksgiving. Piper then explains that he has reached the conclusion that there are profoundly physical dimensions to some of our mental conditions. In a fallen world, our brains can be subject to brokenness like the rest of our body. Physical means can be used to help people out of their depression, just as medications are gratefully received in the treatment of many other illnesses. In his book, *Healing and the Scriptures*, Martyn Lloyd-Jones, the Welsh doctor and preacher, asks, 'If it is right to use insulin in replacement therapy for the pancreas, why is it wrong to take tablets which influence good chemistry of the brain?'[4]

---

3. John Piper, 'What do you think of Christians taking Anti-Depressants?' (http://www.desiringgod.org/interviews/what-do-you-think-of-christians-taking-antidepressants), accessed 19/03/2021.

4. Quoted on recognizingchrist.com, 'Dr Martyn Lloyd-Jones' Method of Pastoral Care' (http://www.recognizingchrist.com/2014/01/07/dr-marytn-lloyd-jones-method-of-pastoral-care-and-diagnosis/), accessed 19/03/2021.

Chemical imbalances in the brain can lead to anxiety and depression. Similarly, times of grief, trauma and stress can affect the functioning of the brain. Medication may be a temporary measure to restore a person's balance in a time of crisis, or it may be that the person has a disorder like OCD or bipolar that means that they will need long-term medication to help their brain operate in a more balanced manner. Sharon Hastings points out that medication improved her ability to connect with God, freeing her from symptoms which consumed her, and allowing her to gain the stability she needs to practise her faith.

However, medication should not be used as an escape from facing other issues that may be causing you depression and anxiety. These tablets won't take away the scars caused by painful memories. The pain of trauma may need to be worked through with someone who has the relevant experience. If lifestyle issues are contributing to your depression and anxiety, then don't let the relief of medication stop you from addressing the core issues. If your conscience has good reason to be troubled, then a pill won't give you lasting peace.

One pastor changed his opinion on medication for mental health as a result of his own struggles. He began by thinking that Christians should not use medication but just have faith. Then when he started to struggle with his mental health, he decided that while medications might be okay, he was going to battle through without them. After that he came to a place where his mental health had so deteriorated that he accepted the help medication offered. Now, on reflection, he believes that, when used appropriately, we should be thankful for the provision of medication.

Conclusion: Joy is more than a feeling

Many people are too one-dimensional about what a spiritual person looks like. Was the psalmist any less spiritual when he declared that it felt like darkness was his closest friend (Ps. 88:18)? Was Jesus less spiritual when He wept in Gethsemane? The joy of the Lord is very different to simple happiness. It is a deep-rooted confidence that God is in control even when every feeling in our hearts may struggle to take any comfort from that. The spiritual life is not just a matter of passing through this world with a serene smile on your face. The lives of many godly Christians, the experiences of the psalmists, the suffering of our Saviour and the teaching of Scripture all show that one of the ways that we honour God is holding on to Him for dear life in the midst of inner turmoil and pain.

We live in a fallen world, where our brains, like the rest of our body, suffer brokenness and illness. Despite the fact that we had turned our backs on God, He has accepted us as His dearly loved children. Our significance should no longer be in trying to impress the world with our strength but in the fact that we are loved in our weakness. This good news should enable us to be real and vulnerable. We shouldn't feel the need to put on a brave face or act like we are sorted. We can be open about our struggles, which is one of the best things we can do for our mental health. In the next chapter, we are going to see that it really is good to talk.

Let's talk to God as we pray:

Why Lord, do You stand far away? Why are You hiding Yourself from me when I need You more than ever? Can't You see that there are people who make my life miserable? They have no time for You, but their lives seem easier than mine. They seem to think that they can do what they want, for You will do nothing. Lord God, don't forget those of us who are in distress! I know that You are a father to those who have no one to help them. I know that You will listen to my prayers. You will turn your ear to me. You hear the pain of my heart. You will bring justice for those who have been mistreated. Amen.

(Adapted from Psalm 10)

4

IS IT WORTH TELLING PEOPLE
HOW WE FEEL?

'Mental pain is less dramatic than physical pain, but it is far more common and also more hard to bear. The frequent attempt to conceal mental pain increases the burden: it is easier to say, "My tooth is broken" than to say, "My heart is broken."'[1]
(C. S. Lewis)

Michaela's anxieties started when she was in her teens. Her worries centred on whether she really was a Christian. However, these anxieties later turned into dark and intrusive thoughts. She didn't think that this was mental illness. Her fears made sense to her, even if they would have seemed ridiculous to others. As the pressure of these thoughts grew to crisis level, a friend encouraged her to go to the doctor. She didn't want to. She just wanted the thoughts to go away. She didn't want to validate those thoughts

---

1. C. S. Lewis, *The Problem of Pain* (London: William Collins, 1940), p. 161.

by talking about them. But eventually she could take no more. The anxiety had become all-encompassing. She agreed to get help.

Three years later Michaela is open about the fact that she has OCD. It took time to come to terms with being ill. It took time to be comfortable telling people. She explains that it makes you feel vulnerable. It opens you to misunderstanding. But being open about her illness makes her feel more real, she can identify more with people's brokenness and it's a relief not to have to put on a face.

In this chapter I want to encourage you to talk about your struggles with depression and anxiety. Being open will help you get the support and help that you need. In fact, the gospel of grace enables you to be vulnerable because your security is not supposed to be based on what people think about you, but on the steadfast love of the God who knows you and who understands your brokenness.

IT IS NOT UNUSUAL TO STRUGGLE WITH DEPRESSION AND ANXIETY

One Sunday evening we had a service looking at the issue of mental health. After I had talked, I asked a neurologist, Elijah Chaila, to do a question and answer session. Elijah reminded us of the need to talk. Talk to your loved ones and tell them how you feel. Talk to your pastor and people in your church. Seek help and support. It is really important that you feel free to talk to your doctor, he advised.

Being open about your mental health won't always be easy. I tend to be an open person, but I still don't always feel comfortable saying that I have obsessive-compulsive disorder. I don't want to appear odd, and mental illnesses can come with unhelpful stereotypes (just think of some of the OCD portrayals in movies like *As Good as it Gets* where Jack Nicholson plays a very odd man who is supposedly struggling with this disorder).

During our question and answer session with Elijah, two young men from different countries of origin claimed that in their cultures people don't get depressed. Since then, I have heard depression being referred to as a white-man's illness or a Western thing. Elijah told me that in Zambia, where he is from, depression is such a neglected subject that there isn't even a word for it in his language. However, World Health Organization research shows that depression and anxiety are not simply a Western issue. I would suggest that in cultures where there is a greater stigma around mental health, there are many more people suffering their own isolated inner turmoil than are noticed by others in their society, and that this isolation only adds to their pain.

Sadly, such stigma can exist in the church. I had one friend tell me that he thought it was a mistake that I told the church that I had had a breakdown. He thought that if I had simply explained that I was sick, then people might have concluded that I was suffering from the flu! He's a good friend who meant well. He was trying to protect me from gossip, but it was a reminder of how some people view problems with mental health. Don't let people's attitudes stop you from experiencing the support that comes through being open about the nature of your suffering. You will find that most people are very supportive and many of those who say insensitive things don't actually mean any harm! The benefits of being open will far outweigh the costs of keeping your suffering to yourself.

It may be that God will use your openness to help others. When I was in a dark place, a friend at a small group blurted out, 'Paul, I am so glad that you struggle with depression.' She did not mean to be insensitive. I knew what she meant. She felt that she could relate her own brokenness to me because I too struggled. As she later explained, 'it makes you human.' Being open about your depression and anxiety may make you a safe person for other people to be open with.

It is hard to overestimate the value of a caring friend who will listen, and with whom you can be open. I had one friend who showed such patience with me as I emailed him almost every day during my time of intense depression and anxiety. I had other friends who had to do little more than ask me how I was with such a genuine heart that I felt love and support. I even used to go walking with my friend, Andy, who was going through a bad patch at the same time that I was very anxious and depressed. We were miserable together, but we were also an encouragement to each other. We shared a fellowship of suffering.

However, when you are going through a time of particularly difficult depression and anxiety there may be people that you need to keep a distance from. There may be those who put too much of an emotional burden upon you or who are very insensitive to how you are feeling. When my mental health is struggling, I tend to keep a safe distance from people who are too 'in your face' or who are very intense. You may need to avoid those who simply want to try and fix you. You may even find that some types of prayer ministry do you more harm than good. Don't feel guilty about this. You don't have to take everyone's advice. You are not the only person who is called to bear the burdens of others. It might not be your time to try to be there for everybody.

WHEN SHOULD I TALK TO THE PROFESSIONALS?

It was only after years of struggling with depression and anxiety that I went and talked to a doctor. I think I should have gone much earlier. You might be wondering if this is something that you should do. I asked a GP friend about his views on when it was the right time to seek the help of a medical professional. Tim began by saying that you should definitely go if you have suicidal thoughts or physical symptoms. Among those physical symptoms he included self-neglect, not eating and severe sleeping problems. He also would encourage you to go if you are finding yourself coping with your emotional pain through dependency on such things as increased alcohol intake or drugs. He points out that you should not worry about talking to your doctor about your emotions and thoughts because they are likely to have dealt with similar cases and aren't easily shocked. Similarly, a friend who is a trained counsellor told me that he always encourages people to seek professional help if they feel they need to. He considers that in some cases people make their situation worse when they delay going. There is nothing to be lost in going to the doctor even if you are not sure your case warrants it. It is better to be safe than sorry.

IT IS NOT A BAD WITNESS TO BE HONEST WITH THE PROFESSIONALS

After I was first diagnosed with OCD, I underwent a course in cognitive behaviour therapy. CBT addresses thoughts, feelings and behaviours. It aims to challenge those thoughts that are unhelpful to our emotions and replace them with more positive ones. CBT doesn't delve into your past to examine some of the roots of why you are struggling, but it does give you coping skills and tools to function. I decided that I was going to be totally transparent with my therapist. I discussed embarrassing thoughts and even struggles with sin. I am glad I did. Your therapist or counsellor will see through it if you are trying to present them with the image of being some sort of super-saint. Besides, there is a great testimony in being able to say, 'I am not a Christian because I have it together; I am a Christian because God is forgiving and kind.' Our testimony is not about how good we are but about the good God who passionately loves His struggling and imperfect children. This openness may be the most refreshing thing that they have ever experienced in someone who claims to be religious. I always tell people not to feel they are compromising their Christian witness as they open up with a counsellor. They are witnessing to a God who is full of amazing grace.

My friend Brenda, a lecturer in psychology, told me that research shows that the key ingredient for successful counselling and therapy depends on the 'therapeutic alliance'. The therapeutic alliance is the relationship you have with your counsellor or therapist. I had the benefit of having a great therapist with whom I felt completely at ease. When I asked Brenda her opinion on whether someone should go to a Christian or a secular counsellor, she pointed out that while secular counselling can be very beneficial, it does leave out the spiritual side of your life, and it may be easier to form a therapeutic alliance with someone who shares your worldview. Of course, it might not be possible to find a Christian cognitive behaviour therapist or counsellor in your area or find one that you can afford. In the Republic of Ireland, where I live, they are very scarce. Take the help that is available to you. Although, if you find that your therapist is not open to your beliefs, then you may need to seek another.

Conclusion

I have watched Michaela come to terms with her illness. She is a close friend. She is a mission worker in Limerick, and I was so delighted the day that I saw her prayer letter on the missionary noticeboard in our church containing the news that she had been struggling with OCD. It was there for all to see. This was not a sign of failure, but the words of someone who was witnessing to the world that her faith is not based on having her life sorted, but that she is living as a child of her Heavenly Father in a world that is fallen. It is a testimony that her faith is based on His strength, not hers. The Christian gospel enables us to be vulnerable with people because we know that our acceptance by God is secure. It is a great misrepresentation of the gospel to pretend that you are always strong. The Christian should not be ashamed of the fact that they struggle with their mental health. There is nothing wrong with being broken in this fallen world. All of us are broken in some way or other. The apostle Paul boasted in his weaknesses (2 Cor. 12:9).

It is good to talk to people, and it is even more important to talk to God. In the next chapter I want to think about prayer and other ways we put our faith into practice to help us as we struggle.

Let's pray to the God who wants us to be real with Him:

O Lord, You have searched me, and You know me. You know my thoughts before I think them. You know my words before they are on my tongue. You know my motives and my loves. Even though You see what is not good in me, You are forgiving and gracious. You will always be with me, and You will never let me go. You made me in my mother's womb. You never take Your loving eyes off me. Your plans are always for my good. Help me when I need to grow through pain. I will not forget that You are kind. Amen.

(Adapted from Psalm 139)

5

How can God help me in the midst of this pain?

'Pursuing maturity, rather than happiness, has changed the way I think about my life … it allows me room to find joy in the midst of all seasons.'[1]
(Chris Cipollone)

Luisa had just reached a stage in her struggles with depression where she had to take time off. She had not done this before, and she felt guilty. She shouldn't have felt guilty. She needed time to recover. She badly needed space from work. One time I asked Luisa what got her through her times of depression. She replied, 'Prayer, the support of friends and family, and knowing that the tears won't last forever. The thought that heaven's gates are already open for me is so comforting. The thought of being immensely loved by God. I also try to remember that I was in a bad place before and eventually got out of it.'

---

1. Chris Cipollone, *Down Not Out: Depression, Anxiety, and the Difference Jesus Makes* (The Good Book Company, 2018), p. 63.

I asked another friend the same question. Sheila replied, 'Sometimes it's to walk down the [canal] bank and watch all the wildlife. The thing that really gets me through is to know that "this too will pass", even though it does not feel like that. Also, God is taking me through this to teach me something, i.e. to have more compassion and empathy for the people I come across who are hurting. I can turn all my experiences into good.'

Christians have to endure the pain of living in a fallen world. But we do not have to do this alone. Our Heavenly Father may allow us to pass through times of sorrow and stress, but He is always with us. He asks His people: 'Can a mother forget the baby at her breast and have no compassion on the child she has borne? Though she may forget, I will not forget you' (Isa. 49:15). God wants us to lean on Him as we listen to His Word and speak to Him in prayer; as we allow His love to flow through us to others and cause our hearts to grow; as we refuse to drive ourselves into the ground but work from a place of rest; and as we are loved by His people.

LISTEN TO HIM THROUGH HIS WORD AND SPEAK TO HIM IN PRAYER

The Psalms of lament are a God-given resource for those who are depressed and anxious. Try out Psalm 13 for size (it's my favourite). These laments are shockingly raw in their honesty and the psalmists are not afraid to cry out to God with their questions and complaints. Often in these psalms there is a movement from despair to hope. This can be the Christian's experience as we pray. In the midst of our pain a little hope begins to shine. But the psalmists are also aware that this won't always be the case. In Psalm 88, there is nothing but darkness. The psalmist ends with the declaration that darkness is his closest friend. Prayer is not a quick fix to simply feeling better. Sometimes heaven seems silent.

During my time of dark depression, I was actually greatly helped by a psalm that is not a lament, Psalm 103. This psalm reminded me of the tender love and forgiveness of our Father God. If you are travelling through a crisis at the moment, it might be a help to take small pieces of Scripture and try to ponder them for the day. One friend shared with me that Romans 5:3-5 are life verses for her, and that they get her through lonely and hard times. These verses say, 'we also glory in our sufferings, because we know that suffering produces perseverance; perseverance, character; and character, hope. And hope does not put us to shame, because God's love has been poured out into our hearts through the Holy Spirit, who has been given to us.' If you were to ask my friend David for his life-verse he would say, 'Whoever dwells in the shelter of the Most High, will rest in the shadow of the Almighty' (Ps. 91:1).

When you are struggling it may be good to take one of the four gospels and dwell on the compassion of Jesus. Or what about reading and rereading the story of the gracious father and his two wayward sons (Luke 15:11-32)? A short and grace-filled book like Ruth, Jonah or Philippians may be helpful when your concentration is struggling. I know of one psychiatrist who did an in-depth study of Hosea during a time of depression because he wanted to drill the message of God's love deep into his aching heart.

We listen to God, but we also talk to Him. The problem for me was that when I was in the pits I could not pray with much focus. I tended to go around and around in circles just asking God to make me better. 'Help me, Lord; help me, Lord; help me, Lord.' I found it hard to make much progress beyond such thoughts. I am not great at prayer at the best of times. At one stage I started typing out prayers on my computer to give them more direction. That actually helped me.

Don't feel guilty about how hard you are finding it to pray when you are anxious and depressed. Your Heavenly Father understands. Cast your anxieties upon Him, even when you are struggling to believe that He cares for you. He is kind and gracious. Set realistic and helpful prayer goals. Don't blame yourself for the fact that God seems absent. He is not absent, even though your feelings tell you He is. Ask people to pray for you and pray with you. Remember that prayer does actually change things.

Throughout my life I have kept a journal on and off. I found it really helpful to write a journal when I was going through that crisis of depression and anxiety. Journaling helped me express myself. I tended not to write entries about what I was doing each day but processed some of the thoughts that were troubling me. I journaled on issues like doubt and my question of the relationship between the love and justice of God. You could use your journal to write out prayers or helpful verses of Scripture. Journaling can be raw and real but try to use your entries to move your thinking in a positive direction. Journaling actually gave me hope that one day I would look back on my entries from a happier place. As it turns out, I have.

ALLOW GOD'S LOVE TO FLOW THROUGH YOU AND SO ENLARGE YOUR HEART

When I looked on the National Health Service (UK) website[2] for helpful things for mental health, they emphasise the mental health benefit of doing things for other people. They explain that even the smallest act can count whether it is a smile, a thank you or a kind word. They also point to the mental health benefits of volunteering. Perhaps there is an area of service in your church you could be involved in that could benefit you as you are a benefit to others. It is always important for us to let our faith challenge us to love other people. You may not be able to do much when you are very depressed and anxious; however, there is healing power in doing things for others in the love of God. Depression and anxiety can have the effect of making you more empathetic to others who suffer pain in their lives.

I remember going through a time of deep anxiety before my first-year college exams. It was the first time I had struggled with fears of having committed the unforgivable sin and I was depressed and fearful. I went for a walk through the streets of Dublin to gather my thoughts. There in a doorway was a homeless young man sheltering in his makeshift cardboard bed. I can't say that I know how awful that must be, but I know that in my suffering I felt for him in a way that I am not sure I would have previously. Pain can make us more compassionate and empathetic. When you have the strength, let that compassion move you to appropriate action. Always let it move you to prayer.

---

2. National Health Service, '5 Steps to mental wellbeing' (http://www.nhs.uk/mental-health/self-help/guides-tools-and-activities/five-steps-to-mental-wellbeing/), accessed 19/03/2021.

Listen to the healing words of Isaiah 58:10: '… and if you spend yourselves on behalf of the hungry and satisfy the needs of the oppressed, then your light will rise in the darkness, and your night will become like the noonday.' There is a spiritual dynamic at work when we serve other people in the name of God. We look for God's help to love well and as His love flows through us, it enlarges our heart. We love because God first loved us (1 John 4:19). It actually helps to try to take our thoughts off our own worries and consider how we might show God's kindness to others.

DON'T DRIVE YOURSELF INTO THE GROUND BUT WORK FROM A PLACE OF REST

Rest is a major theme in the Bible. In the Old Testament God gave His people a weekly day of rest. In the New Testament Jesus invited the people to Himself saying: 'Come to me, all you who are weary and burdened, and I will give you rest' (Matt. 11:28). Jesus was telling the people to stop working to earn God's acceptance and to humble themselves and receive His eternal life as a gift. The theme of rest finds its fulfilment in heaven, where we shall rest from our labours (Rev. 14:13). We should be seeking to live a life of meaningful work (not necessarily paid employment) and satisfying rest.

When we were first married, Caroline told me I was working too hard. I wanted to say 'thanks!' It was as if I did not realise that it is disobedient to God not to refresh ourselves through rest. An unwillingness to take proper rest is a failure of faith. It may reveal that we are motivated by pride (as I was and often still am) or that we think God can't do without us. As one friend wisely told me, 'We are to work from a place of rest, not rest from a place of work'.

Hear Jesus inviting you to take some time aside. Meditate on the story of Mary and Martha (Luke 10:38-42). See how Jesus sought to refresh Himself in prayer (Luke 4:42). I tend to forget about God during my day off and just relax, but that is to miss the main purpose of time for rest and the main source of true refreshing. Incorporate spiritual refreshment into your rest days. Make as many changes in your lifestyle as possible to ensure that you can cope. Learn to say 'no' without feeling guilty. Make sure that you get enough sleep.

It is important to have things in life that you are looking forward to. When you are depressed and anxious you might find it hard to enjoy anything. But it is helpful to keep doing things that you would normally enjoy. During my last dark patch, Caroline and I tried to go for lunch once a week (I might not have had much of an appetite, and I was not great company, but it helped us stay close). After I had to take time off a number of years ago, I revisited my work and life balance. As a result, for a number of years I went to the cinema on my own for a Monday afternoon treat. I found it very relaxing. Some antidepressant medications can lower your libido, but it is important that a married couple don't neglect making the effort to keep this aspect of their relationship alive.

The apostle Paul told his young disciple, Timothy, that bodily training is of some value (1 Tim. 4:8). We must not ignore the connection between the body and the soul. I know people who get huge emotional benefit from walking, jogging and cycling. These activities release endorphins in your brain that will make you feel relaxed and a bit more positive. It is particularly helpful to walk in a beautiful place like a forest or along some other route where you can enjoy nature. Walking on your own can give you space to relax. I struggle with a little bit of social anxiety and find that going for a walk with someone is a great way to catch up with them as it is less intense than having to sit face to face.

TRY NOT TO STOP GOING TO CHURCH
During times of anxiety and depression it is tempting to stop going to church. Church can be very hard to go to when you are not feeling well. You may not enjoy people fussing over how you are. You may dread all the small talk that takes place at the coffee time after the service. You might find the music too cheery and struggle to concentrate during the talk. But it is good to be with God's people. You might be surprised how God uses the words of a song or sermon to speak to you. You will be reminded that these people in your church family love you. If church seems a real struggle then, for a time, it might be a good idea to arrive just as the service starts and leave before coffee time. If you get out of the habit of going to church you may later find it hard to get back into the habit of going.

CONCLUSION: GROWING IN THE SORROW AND STRESS
Last summer I went on our family holiday believing that I should have made a full recovery from my breakdown. The problem was that I was not entirely well. I was still struggling with dark thoughts. This frustrated the life out of me. I was not content to still be suffering. I wanted to

be perfectly well. A year later, I am writing these words just a few weeks from the same family holiday time. If I am honest, I am not entirely better. There is still slight residual depression and anxiety lingering over me. But I am okay with it. I am not demanding complete healing, and that helps me to be content. God's great goal for our life is not that we are always happy but that we are becoming more like Jesus. I actually found it helpful when an experienced pastor friend suggested that God might have a purpose for me in continuing to struggle with my mental health. We might honour God most as we lean on Him in the midst of our pain. I am not saying that you should not make every effort to get well. I am saying that we should not want to trade our life for a different one. Comparing our life to a seemingly easier one will only make us discontented.

We are called to lean on God in our pain. But what if we fear that God isn't willing to hold us up? It is not unusual to hear a Christian say that they don't know how anyone goes through depression and anxiety without a knowledge of our Heavenly Father. But what if our illness is robbing us of belief in His love? I have met a number of depressed and anxious Christians who worry that God has not accepted them. I have struggled with a lack of assurance that I am a Christian, and in particular I feared that I was beyond the mercy of God. In the next chapter we will see that God wants you to know His acceptance and He wants you to be secure in the knowledge that you belong to Him.

Let's pray to the God who listens:

My God, my God, why have You forsaken me? Why are You so far from lifting these feelings of despair? It's like I cry out to You every day and You don't hear my groaning. I have enough people who don't understand what I am going through. Please tell me You are not like that too. I can't find any rest from my pain, either day or night. Even when I hide under the covers in bed, I can't get away from my worries and sorrow. I know that some are saying that I don't have faith, but I do trust You. I am just so tired of this. When I get through this, I am going to tell everyone that You are good. For I do know that You care. I know that better days lie ahead. Don't let me lose hope! In the morning, when the pain is worst, help me remember that Your compassions never fail, they are new every morning, great is Your faithfulness. Amen.

(Adapted from Psalm 22)

6

How can I be sure I am forgiven when I feel so guilty?

'A man may be a true believer and yet would give all the world, were it in his power, to know that he is a believer.'[1]
(Thomas Brooks, 1654)

In his book, *Spiritual Depression*, the great doctor and preacher, Martyn Lloyd-Jones, has a chapter on 'that one sin'. He says people came to him with guilt about a past sin that haunted them, more than any other issue. In this chapter I want to deal with the issue of guilt and forgiveness. Feelings of guilt can lead to mental health issues such as anxiety, and the gospel offers more than a superficial solution.

In my own Christian life, I have gone through times when I have feared that I was beyond God's forgiveness. Indeed, almost every Christian, at some time in their life, has struggled with the worry that they are not really

---

1. Thomas Brooks, *Heaven on Earth* (Edinburgh: The Banner of Truth Trust, 1961), p. 15.

a child of the Father. Sometimes this lack of assurance can produce a numbness, but other times there can be panic and fear.

In this chapter we will look at forgiveness and assurance.

FEARING YOU ARE BEYOND GOD'S FORGIVENESS

John Bunyan, the author of *Pilgrim's Progress*, feared that he was beyond God's forgiveness. He writes about this in his book *Grace Abounding to the Chief of Sinners*. Bunyan often rambles in this book, and some have suggested that it may reveal that he had OCD. This book is a classic for those who are desperate to know God's forgiveness. He deals with every objection to God's forgiveness and takes great comfort from the promise of Jesus who says, '… whoever comes to me I will never drive away' (John 6:37).

Similarly, the slave-trader turned hymn-writer, John Newton, struggled for a while with the fear that he was beyond God's forgiveness. In particular he worried about the warning passages in the book of Hebrews that speak of people falling away beyond recovery.

Newton had rejected the faith his mother had taught him. His blasphemous language and cursing shocked even the most hardened of his fellow sailors. He argued with those who claimed to be Christians and successfully convinced one young man to pack in his faith. He did things on those slave-ships that he later decided were too crude to mention in his autobiography. But during a storm in the Atlantic he cried out to the God he had denied and truly became a Christian.

Initially, after turning to Christ, he wondered how God could forgive a wretch like him. Assurance that he was now a child of God didn't come to him straight away. But it did come, and he became a most compassionate pastor to many struggling people.

PEOPLE WHO GROW UP IN CHRISTIAN HOMES CAN HAVE PROBLEMS WITH ASSURANCE

When people grow up in a church culture that places great emphasis on testimonies of conversion (the more dramatic the better), people can struggle to be sure they are a Christian because there is no obvious 'before and after' contrast in their life. I have heard people say that they wished they had become a Christian from a life of disrepute so that they would then have an obvious comparison of the change that had been brought about in their lives. Other people growing up in churches where there is an emphasis on identifying the moment of conversion struggle because they can't be sure when they did respond to God's grace. They can't state a date and time when they appeared to travel from spiritual death to spiritual life.

The reality of your faith is not dependent on having some terrible past or knowing the hour you prayed a prayer of commitment but on the fact that you currently depend on Jesus for grace and life, and that you want Him to go on transforming you.

I have also found that fear concerning the warning passages in Hebrews about falling away can be particularly a factor for those who grew up in Christian homes and made a profession of faith at an early stage in life. Their problem centres on the fact that their greatest sins and times of rebellion against God have come after they have supposedly become a Christian. They may struggle with the memories of behaviour that took place in adolescence and later teen years. They know that God forgives everything that we do before we are brought into His family, but they worry about things they did after they claimed to belong to Him. They fail to realise that what is being talked about in these warning passages is a hardness of heart that would make any sincere desire to repent impossible.

Don't refuse to take God at His Word

When people came to him about 'that one sin' Martyn Lloyd-Jones would bring them to 1 John 1:9, which assures us that if we confess our sin, God will forgive us our sins and cleanse us from all unrighteousness. He would then explain to the distressed person that 'this is a categorical statement made by the Holy Spirit through His servant. There is no limit to it … I cannot see any qualifications whatsoever. Whatever your sin – it is as wide as that – it does not matter what it was.' The person's real problem, he diagnosed, was not the past sin they were worrying about but the fact that they were refusing to take God at His Word. He would tell them to have faith in the promises of God.

Your problem may be deeper than any issue of sin

I have compiled a full copybook of commentary quotes that back up what Lloyd-Jones and others teach about the certainty of God's forgiveness to all who truly repent. When a friend of mine shared with me that she experienced the same fears, I gave it to her. But it didn't actually give her much help. Why was that? It was because my friend's problem was the same as mine; she was struggling with chronic anxiety. She too struggles with OCD.

Could it be that your inability to feel peace in God's promises has a deeper root than you realise? Could there be reasons why you fear that God would never accept you? Could it be that you have a distorted view of God? Are there memories of rejection that you are projecting onto your relationship with Him? Have you gone to a church where God has been presented as petty, vindictive and reluctant to forgive? Are you by nature and by nurture prone to feelings of insecurity? Might you have problems with an anxiety disorder that contributes to an unhealthy fear of God? You might obsess about your rebellion and sin, but Jesus promises us that God never turns away anyone who comes to Him in sincere repentance (John 6:37). You will tell me that you fear that your repentance isn't sincere, but all of our repentance is imperfect. While you may be scared that you do not love God, your desire to love Him is itself given by God.

Objecting to assurance

The promises of God are the most important means of seeking assurance. But the New Testament emphasises two other means for helping us see that we belong to God: the witness of the Spirit and the change that God brings to the life of the Christian. However, a tendency to anxiety and depression can cause us to doubt these as well.

The anxious person may struggle to feel the witness of the Spirit because their anxiety is causing their feelings to be all over the place. The depressed person may feel numb and so wonder why they don't have more passion for God. This does not mean that the Spirit is not pouring His love into their heart (Rom. 5:5) but that they are simply struggling to experience Him. This can be particularly painful if you are involved in church circles that place an emphasis on emotions. Don't let this worry you. Nowhere in the New Testament does it say that you have to feel assured that you are a Christian to be a Christian. Love for God is not measured by your emotions. Ask God to help you deal with the emotional pain that causes you to doubt His love so that you can know the peace the Spirit wants you to enjoy.

If you have grown up in a harsh and legalistic church, you may struggle to believe that your life shows enough evidence of having been born again. You may tend to always notice your failures and yet be blind to anything good that God is doing in your life. Maybe there is a sin that you are having trouble mastering and so you feel defeated. You need to keep in mind that the Christian is not a flawless person. In fact, if someone thinks they no longer sin they are deceived (1 John 1:8). We are a work in progress. We have a heart that is still under construction. You may not be what you would like to be, but neither are you what you once were.

God is the one who gives people a desire to know Him. He is the one who causes people to do what Jesus commands and avoid what Jesus forbids. It is evidence of the work of the Holy Spirit when you are aware your repentance is shallow and long for a pure heart. He is the one who causes you to want to serve Him with gladness. This is evidence of God at work in a person's life. Without the work of the Holy Spirit you would be opposed to the gospel of grace (Rom. 8:7). Without the work of the Holy Spirit you would be trying to prove that you are essentially a good person. Without the work of the Holy Spirit you wouldn't want Jesus to be the central reality in your life. Often your friends have less doubts about the change God has brought about in your life than you do and it's not because they don't really know what you are like. It's because people can be more objective when they view things from a little distance.

WHAT SHOULD YOU DO IF YOU ARE STRUGGLING WITH ASSURANCE?

I knew a young man who had only met his father once, and that meeting did not go well. Understandably he had real trouble believing that his Heavenly Father accepted him. I would suggest that you consider the possibility that your lack of assurance might be related to issues that go beyond your past sin and current failure.

It may be that issues with depression and anxiety contribute to these worries about assurance, as these worries about assurance may contribute to your depression and anxiety. You may need to stop examining your sin and failures under a microscope and start getting help for underlying issues causing anxiety. You may need to stop constantly seeking reassurance about the sins that cause you to doubt the reality of your faith. It may be that your worries about assurance won't pass away quickly. It may take years. There may be times when your anxieties get the better of you and you obsess over these issues. However, have hope. God wants you to know that you are a Christian (1 John 5:13). Your assurance will grow over time.

Peter Orr, my wonderful friend who I regularly emailed for reassurance during my dark depression, at times had the wisdom to ignore my specific questions and try to get me to focus on the promises of God. That is what I want you to do before we finish this chapter. I pray that as you think about these promises you may have the strength to move beyond the emotional issues that make it so hard to accept the promises. Why not spend some time meditating on the following and ask the Holy Spirit to bring such healing to your mind and emotions that the promises would become a source of joy and confidence?

> Psalm 32:5: 'Then I acknowledged my sin to you and did not cover up my iniquity. I said, "I will confess my transgressions to the Lord." And you forgave the guilt of my sin.'
>
> Psalm 51:17: 'My sacrifice, O God, is a broken spirit; a broken and contrite heart you, God, will not despise.'
>
> John 3:36: 'Whoever believes in the Son has eternal life...'
>
> John 6:37: 'All those the Father gives me will come to me, and whoever comes to me I will never drive away.'
>
> 1 John 1:9: 'If we confess our sins, he is faithful and just and will forgive us our sins and purify us from all unrighteousness.'

What sort of father wouldn't want his children to feel safe in his love and know that they are a part of the family? God is a good father who wants people to come into His family and to be secure in His steadfast acceptance. His wonderful promises of grace are designed so that we might feel loved and secure. Dwelling on the promises of God is a good thing for the Christian to do.

CONCLUSION

I came up with a slogan that I thought was clever (until I found out that many people have said the exact same thing before me). I said to the congregation at the end of a sermon, 'Your problem is not so much that you don't love God enough (although none of us love Him as much as we ought), but that you don't realise how much God loves you.' That is one of the tragedies when we struggle to believe that God has accepted us, delights in us and will never let us go. I used to pray, 'Lord, I would throw myself upon You, but I am scared You won't catch me.' I feared He would let me crash to the ground.

There is a life-transforming power in seeing a glimpse of how much God cares for you. My sense of assurance is far from perfect, but it has grown beyond measure. Look at your own sin and you will see many reasons why He should not accept you; look to the cross and you will see the lengths to which He has gone to win you for Himself. Think of the father of the prodigal son who sprints through the village to meet him and repeatedly kisses him. He will never turn you away no matter how far you have strayed. You may not realise it, but it was His love that brought you home.

It is a tragedy when a Christian does not realise how much the Father loves them. Continue seeking to trust God for assurance that you belong to Him. It is also a tragedy when someone loses all sense of hope. This can be a very dangerous place to be. In the next chapter I want to look at the very sensitive issue of suicide.

Let's pray to the God of mercy:

'Have mercy on me, because You are loving. Forgive me, because You are gracious. Help me remember that the blood of Jesus goes on cleansing me from all my wickedness' (1 John 1:7). I am so racked with feelings of guilt and regret. The thing that hurts me most is that I have let You down. I want You to change me from within. I know that You promise to forgive. You will not turn me away. You are the one who gives me the desire to repent, and You will accept that repentance. Show me that You delight to welcome home the prodigal. I would try to prove myself to You, but You just want me to depend on You. I realise that my worries about Your acceptance may be rooted in deeper wounds and stresses. Help me get the help I need. I believe; help me in my unbelief. Amen.

(Adapted from Psalm 51)

7

What about when I don't think I can go on living?

'My experience with depressed people is that when they have suffered from long periods of depression and begin to talk about suicide, we had better pay attention.'[1]
(Curtis Thomas)

I started to write a blog post the day after attending the funeral of a young man, we'll call him Ben, who died by suicide. It was a deeply moving occasion. The speaker was brave enough to talk about how Ben had died, that suicide is never the right thing to do and that the young man who had taken his life had grown up with great parents who loved him deeply. I watched my pastor friend weep with the lad's mother, and I thought: that is the sort of empathy I want to have.

Ben professed to be a Christian and it was not long before someone asked me, 'If a Christian commits suicide, will they go to heaven?' When someone is

---

1. Quoted on A Christ-follower with a Limp, 'Suicide: Shattered Hearts', September 27, 2020. (http://pastorscottcarson.blogspot.com/2020/09/suicide-shattered-hearts.html), accessed 19/03/2021.

brought to faith in Christ the verdict that God places over them is 'now no condemnation' (Rom. 8:1). That verdict stands even when the Christian sins. God holds on to His people even when they fall and fail. I am not saying that sin does not matter. In fact, if you think sin does not matter to God you probably don't know Him. It is never right for a Christian to take their own life.

I am aware that Ben suffered from deep anxiety. I know that he had no intention of hurting anyone and he was not seeking to rage against God. He had simply lost all sense of hope and felt that he could not live with the pain. Indeed, many people who die by suicide think that those they love would be better off without them. Sadly, in the midst of their despair, many Christians struggle to know that God cares for them too.

Jesus is a compassionate man of sorrow who was familiar with grief (Isa. 53:3), who knew such anguish that He despaired of life (Matt. 26:38). Nevertheless, He says that we are not to take life (Luke 18:20), not even our own. He longs for you to access the truth that God will never forsake you if you trust in Him (Heb. 13:5). He longs to hold you in your pain and bring you through the storm. Of course, I'm not naïve. I realise that even we who trust the Lord can find ourselves in a place where darkness seems our closest friend and that darkness feels like it will never lift (Ps. 88:18). But in the midst of that darkness we should be trying to honour Jesus and resisting the temptation to do what He forbids.

My country, Ireland, has a bad historical record of how it dealt with suicide. Those who died by suicide were excluded from the 'holy ground' within a graveyard. How harsh such thinking was. We must deal with this issue in a way that reflects our compassionate and gracious Saviour.

The city of Limerick where I live has a painful prevalence of suicide. Drive through the city any weekend and you will see people patrolling the River Shannon ready to talk with those who are contemplating a jump. Everyone in this city knows the sound of the rescue helicopter as it circles the city and what you mean when you say 'someone went into the river'. In such a dark society, Christians need to be people of light. To those who are racked with guilt, we can talk of how Jesus came into the world to save sinful people like us. To those who despair, we can speak of a love that will never let us go. We must seek to befriend the isolated and lonely.

As I attended Ben's funeral, I thought back to the couple of times in my life when I felt hopeless and anxious. I am sure that my pain was not as dark as his was. I couldn't say that I was suicidal. Yet I do remember wanting to die. Now I am glad I didn't. Now I can look back from a much happier place. That's what makes the funeral of a suicide victim so tragic. If only they could have made it through that day, that week, that month or that year. If he had lived, I think he would have come to a place where he was glad to be alive.

AN IRREVERSIBLE ACTION TO SOLVE A TEMPORARY PROBLEM

Rick Warren is a famous pastor in America whose son, Matthew, died by suicide. He says to those who are contemplating suicide, you need to remember that you are taking an irreversible action to solve a temporary problem.[2] Most suicidal people do not want to end their life; rather they want to end their pain. Suicide is not the way to do this. Warren points out that the emotions you are feeling will pass. No emotion lasts forever. You will not always feel the way you do now. Indeed, even if the pain doesn't lift, you are called to honour Jesus by resisting suicidal temptations. Warren also reminds us that God does not want you to travel through the pressures you are facing on your own. Find someone who cares and tell them how you feel. Never try to face suicidal feelings on your own.

YOU NEED TO REMEMBER GRACE IF YOU HAVE LOST A LOVED ONE TO SUICIDE

You need to hear the gospel if you have a loved one who has died by suicide. A friend who feels guilt over her loved one's death wonders would he have done it if she had been there more for him. God does not want her to live with that guilt. None of us are perfect husbands or wives, parents or children, neighbours or friends. But God wants us to know His forgiveness. Another friend feels angry that her loved one inflicted such pain on her through his death. Such feelings are normal, and need to be worked through; if they are not worked through they will cause more pain. The gospel enables us to forgive the inexcusable in others as the Holy Spirit shows us how God has forgiven the inexcusable in us.

John Newton, the writer of the hymn 'Amazing Grace', was a great friend of the poet William Cowper. Cowper

---

2. In Kathrine Weber, 'Rick Warren: Suicide Is Never the Solution; I Grieve Every Day Over My Son's Fatal Decision' (www.christianpost.com).

struggled with terrible mental health, felt utterly forsaken by God and was often tempted to take his life. Indeed, he tried to on a number of occasions. Newton once wrote to Cowper with the following advice: 'I can only advise you to resist to the utmost every dark and discouraging suggestion …Take encouragement hence to hope that He will not forsake the work of His own hands though He may hide Himself from us for a moment, He has given us a warrant to trust in Him.'[3] Suicide is never the right solution to your pain. For those of you who are grieving a suicide, I hope that you might experience the truth that the psalmist speaks of when he claims that, the Lord is close to the brokenhearted and saves those who are crushed in spirit (Ps. 34:18).

CONCLUSION:
THE DANGER OF BEING MISUNDERSTOOD

One evening I got a series of texts that asked, 'What does God think of suicide?' 'Does it mean that I will go to hell?' 'I am asking because I have nothing to live for!' That text was terrifying. If I gave the wrong answer, would this person take this course of action? I decided to leave aside their question and ask them why they were feeling so low. Thankfully they resisted the urge to harm themselves.

Let me be clear. If you are struggling with suicidal thoughts, suicide is never the right option. It saddens the heart of God and leaves devastation in its wake. As a pastor I have seen the pain it causes. You will cause more damage than you realise. Remember that suicide

---

3. Josiah Bull, *Letters of John Newton* (Edinburgh: The Banner of Truth Trust, 2007), pp. 151-153.

is an irreversible solution to a temporary problem. Many people look back and are glad that they did not act on the impulse to end their life or did not succeed in doing so. You will not always feel low and you will live to be glad that you did not take this way out. Most importantly, if you are a Christian, you want to obey Jesus. He gives life and it is wrong to end the life He gives you. Find people to talk to. Ring a helpline. Talk to your doctor. Contact your pastor, minister or priest. Ask God for the strength not to take this action.

Having spent this entire book so far trying to think of how the depressed and anxious Christian can live for God in a fallen world, I want to turn in the last chapter to those who live alongside those who are struggling with their mental health. How can you care for those you love who are depressed and anxious? As Christians living together as children of the Father in a broken world we are called to bear one another's burdens (Gal. 6:2). To do that, we are going to have to rely on the compassion that the Holy Spirit is willing to pour into our hearts.

Let's pray to the God who is with us in the darkness:

O Lord, the one in whom I have put my trust, why can't I feel You? Why have You allowed my life to come to this? I am crying out to You; listen to me. Why does no one understand how I feel? People look at me and don't know what to say. There is nothing they can do to take away my sorrow. I call out to You, but heaven seems silent! Have You rejected me? I know You haven't. But I am terrified, and I see no light at the end of the tunnel. I am here all alone with my suffering. Lord, come to my help. Though I am overwhelmed with pain I will hold on to You. Though I can't see You, I will trust You. Though You seem far away, I resolve not to disobey You. Amen.

(Adapted from Psalm 88)

8

How can I help those in my church who are depressed and anxious?

'My true friends during this time were the ones I knew were praying for me.'[1]
(Kathryn Greene-McCreight)

The support group, AWARE, states that in the Republic of Ireland one in ten people are suffering the symptoms of depression at any given time.[2] The figures are likely to be similar in the United Kingdom. That being the case, you can be sure that there are probably more people in your church who struggle with depression and anxiety than you realise. Some of them are very good at putting on a smiley face. They may be the last people in the world who you would suspect of being depressed or anxious. Many of them are longing to be helped but are scared of being judged.

How can people in the church help those who struggle with anxiety and depression? How can Christians help

---

1. Kathryn Greene-McCreight, *Darkness is My Only Companion* (Grand Rapids, Michigan: Brazos Press, 2006), p. 53.

2. http://www.aware.ie/information/depression/ accessed 19/03/2021.

their loved ones who are going through this pain? Friends told me that they didn't know what to do when I was ill. It can be hard to know what to say or how to act. You might not know when to make contact or when to give someone space. You may be scared that you will say the wrong thing. The most wonderful thing you can do for them involves loving them when they feel unlovely or unloved, and being patient with them when their progress is slow.

I have come up with a number of suggestions to help you care for those who are struggling with their mental health. If you are reading this chapter to help people who are suffering with anxiety and/or depression I want to say 'thank you for caring'. As the book of Proverbs says, 'A friend loves at all times, and a brother is born for a time of adversity' (Prov. 17:17). The heart of friendship is a willingness to be there for people in their difficulties. At the heart of the church should be a willingness to bear one another's burdens (Gal. 6:2).

Everyone can pray, and prayer is the most important thing we can do.

'Dear friend, I pray that you may enjoy good health and that all may go well with you, even as your soul is getting along well' (3 John 2).

You may know someone who is depressed and anxious but not know what to say to them. You may love someone who is depressed and anxious and not even live near them. Start by talking to God about them. Christians believe that prayer actually changes things and should see prayer as the most important thing that we can do for loved ones.

One of the things that those with mental health issues most need to know is that God loves them. In their pain God can seem absent. The apostle Paul's prayer in the third chapter of Ephesians reminds us that the Holy Spirit reveals to the Christian the extent of God's love for His people. Why not put the name of your depressed friend into that prayer and every morning and evening pray: 'I pray that _____ may have power, together with all God's holy people, to grasp how wide and high and deep is the love of Christ, and to have this love that surpasses knowledge – that he/she may be filled to the measure of all the fullness of God' (adapted from Eph. 3:18-19).

Let them know that you are praying for them, and also tell them that you are willing to pray with them. But do not be forceful about praying with them. They may not feel they know you well enough to be that vulnerable with you. They may not want to be vulnerable at the time you offer. Be available but not pushy. If they do want you to pray with them, begin by asking them exactly how they would like you to pray for them. That will help you pray more specifically into their need.

THERE ARE A VARIETY OF HELPFUL THINGS THAT YOU CAN DO FOR THEM

If you are praying for them then you are doing the most important thing. But there are other things you can do as well. Start by simply being there for them. There can be great healing in being held and having someone simply be there silently. The appropriateness of being present may depend on how well you know the person. They will probably only want to spend a lot of time with their closest friends and family. It is important to respect the privacy of the person's home and so only visit if invited. Ask them out for coffee or tell them you would be happy to call, but only in a way that leaves them free to say no.

If you don't feel close enough to them to spend time with them, then remember that small gestures help. You can write a card, cook a meal, send a text or offer other forms of practical support. During my time of deep depression, I received a wonderfully encouraging card from a friend who knew that I was in pain. It meant so much to me, and I have held on to that card. If you do write to someone make sure that you are clear that you are not expecting a reply from them. You don't want to burden them with an unnecessary responsibility. Kathryn Greene-McCreight writes of her own struggles with bipolar syndrome. Her suffering was severe enough that at times she needed to be hospitalised. She writes: 'The most helpful thing for me were the meals, the offers to do a load of laundry or take care of the children for the afternoon. Even though I often did not accept these offers because of misplaced pride, which depression can foster, knowing that someone cared enough to offer was a source of encouragement.'[3]

Sometimes you will have a clearer awareness that your loved one is suffering from a mental health struggle than they do. Talk to them about your concerns. Encourage them to go to see their doctor. Encourage them to cooperate with the doctor's advice. Your attitude towards medication will affect their willingness to take medication. You may also be aware of times when it seems like the doctors are just throwing medication at them, and you will need to encourage them to deal with some of the root

---

3.   Kathryn Greene-McCreight, *Darkness is My Only Companion,* p. 34.

issues. They may feel nervous about going to a therapist or counsellor, so your support may be needed.

DON'T LET A BIG MOUTH UNDO THE HARD WORK OF ATTENTIVE EARS

If you get the opportunity, listen to those who are suffering. They will be much keener to tell you how they feel than hear your advice about what they should do. They want to be understood and accepted. Ask them perceptive questions. Summarise what you hear them saying, to reassure them you are listening and that you are hearing them. Definitely refrain from interrupting. Then, having done good work with your ears, don't ruin it by being clumsy with your mouth.

Obviously, don't tell them to snap out of it. They would if they could. But this doesn't mean that you don't offer suggestions that might be helpful. Just offer your suggestions modestly, for none of us are experts about what someone else is feeling. As you offer help, be aware of when you are out of your depth. I visited a couple who had heard me speak at a weekend away with their church. One of them had serious mental health struggles. I think they thought I could give more help than I was able to. I quickly realised I didn't know what advice to give. They lived too far away for me to visit regularly and they were getting good pastoral support from their church. I simply urged them to keep visiting their doctor and get whatever professional help they could. I think they were disappointed I couldn't do more for them, but I couldn't and I would have been a fool to try.

Another unhelpful thing to say is 'I know how you feel'. In the last church I pastored, a person came to me and shared how painful they found it when someone belittled their suffering with these words. She doubted that this person did know how she felt. Even if you have suffered from the same type of anxiety or depression, you cannot really know how their depression and anxiety is affecting them, unless you take the time to listen and find out. So, one night I was with the church's pastoral care group. I said to the team, 'I want you to say after me, "I know how you feel". Then, after they said it, I said, "Now, that is the last time I ever want you to use that phrase as part of this team."'

Of course, the good news is that you don't have to have experience of what someone is going through to be a support to them. You just have to be kind and wise. I remember going to a lecturer in a theological college for some help with my depression and anxieties. He was honest enough to say to me that he could not relate to how I felt. He said that he wakes up every morning with a sunny disposition. That's just the way he is. But he was very caring and real. The best thing that you can do for the depressed and anxious is to be a good friend.

You have got to be careful what you say and you have got to be careful how you use the Bible. Firing Bible verses at people can be very unproductive or even counter-productive. Many years ago, a friend of mine, Sarah, suffered a breakdown in her mental health. One of the things that upset her, during this difficult time, was people who would fire Bible verses at her. She knew that 'in all things God works for the good of those who love him' (Rom. 8:28). But it was unhelpful when people who hadn't the love to listen and engage with how she really felt palmed her off with a verse.

That being said, do share the Bible with them. One of the problems when the depressed and anxious begin to miss church is that they are missing the opportunity to be ministered to by God's Word. The sensitive local pastor will always apply the text, conscious of what is going on in the lives of the congregation. But it is not just preachers who have a ministry of the Word. Christians teach each other (Col. 3:16). Therefore, gently share encouraging words that might be a lifting up for the downcast. Rather than trying to fix their problems with a Bible text, talk about what you are learning yourself from the Bible at the moment. Have confidence that the Word gently applied brings healing to the troubled mind.

During my last bout of depression, a friend gave me a puzzled look and exclaimed, 'I don't know what you have to be depressed about.' He meant well, and his words weren't particularly unhelpful. But even if a person's life looks good on the outside, don't underestimate the pain they are feeling on the inside.

The problem with telling people to snap out of it, saying you know how they feel or firing a Bible verse at them, is that in each case you leave the depressed and anxious person with the feeling that you are not willing to engage with their pain. They will feel like you are trying to fix their problem so that you can move on to something else. They are not a problem to be solved. Remember that love is both patient and kind (1 Cor. 13:4). What they need to know is that you are genuinely concerned. Nothing will show them your concern as much as taking the time to listen.

While there are some things not to say, do speak helpful words of encouragement. 'The pleasantness of a friend springs from their heartfelt advice' (Prov. 27:9b). David Murray points out that deep-rooted self-doubt and self-criticism will often emerge and strengthen during a time of depression. Depressed people often feel worthless and useless. But some Christians are reluctant to give people any praise or encouragement because of the risk of making a person proud. However, Murray points out that pride is one of the least risky vices for the person who is depressed. Pride results from having an over-inflated view of oneself. Depression usually involves the opposite. Without minimising the wickedness of the human heart and our inability to please God apart from Christ, 'we should feel free to encourage depressed people to have a more positive view of themselves by highlighting their God-given gifts, their contribution to the lives of others, their usefulness to society, and, if they are Christians, their value to the church.'[4] 'Anxiety weighs down the heart, but a kind word cheers it up' (Prov. 12:25). 'The words of the reckless pierce like swords, but the tongue of the wise brings healing' (Prov. 12:18). 'Gracious words are a honeycomb, sweet to the soul and healing to the bones' (Prov. 16:24).

BE VULNERABLE ABOUT YOUR OWN BROKENNESS

Many years ago, I was in a house when something alerted me that this person might have suffered with OCD. So, I told them about my own struggles with this disorder. The person's face lit up. 'You have OCD? So do I! I have only ever told two people.' What followed was a really enjoyable

---

4. David Murray, *Christians Get Depressed Too* (Grand Rapids, Michigan: Reformed Heritage Books, 2010), pp. 95-96.

conversation about our common experience. Many people want to talk about what is going on inside themselves, but may be fearful to do so. We need to become safe ears for the vulnerable. People will usually feel more free to be open with you if you are open with them.

While not everyone has issues with their mental health, we all have issues. We all have areas of weakness and vulnerability. Vulnerability involves a willingness to be open about the true you that God sees, and not merely present a fake you that you would like everyone else to see. People won't take off their masks with you if you are unwilling to take off your mask with them.

I used to feel a complete fraud giving my testimony in church because I never mentioned my fears, particularly regarding the worries I had about the unforgiveable sin. My insecurity with God meant that I struggled to love Him (I still don't love Him the way I want to). I was scared to be real about these things because I was up at the front in church. I thought that if people knew the real me, they might think I was immature, weak or not a Christian at all. I think that most of us struggle to be real about things like the weakness of our prayer lives, because we are scared that we will be thought of as unspiritual. But we actually want to be known. The gospel of grace is the foundation for vulnerability. True vulnerability has community-transforming power. We are a community of failed and imperfect people known and loved by our gracious Heavenly Father.

I was talking to a friend about his anxieties and realised that his intrusive thoughts might be an indication that he had OCD. I thought, 'How do I talk about this without him thinking that I believe he is odd?' So, I told him about the fact that I struggle with similar types of thoughts. When I told him about the help I had received, he was encouraged. We need to figure out how to speak to people about anxiety and depression in a way that doesn't leave them feeling strange. We speak as one broken person to another. The truth is that depression and anxiety are very common and normal experiences. As David Murray says, 'Depression is a normal abnormality.'

MODEL THE KINDNESS AND GRACE OF GOD

Depressed and anxious people need to know that God is good and kind. They may draw conclusions about God's nature from watching those who claim to know Him. When those who are thought of as being the established Christians in a church are harsh and severe, then the sensitive will begin to think that God is unapproachable and mean. When Christians are overly critical, then God will be thought of as disapproving. So, try to show them the kindness of God through your life. Be humble about your dependence on God's mercy and grace. Show them the gospel through your attitude. 'Let your gentleness be evident to all' (Phil. 4:5). 'Be merciful to those who doubt' (Jude 22). 'Be completely humble and gentle; be patient, bearing with one another in love' (Eph. 4:2).

Visiting someone from our church in hospital one evening, she said to me, 'I met a really nice doctor here. He was so kind. I think he might be a Christian.' I thought I knew who she was talking about and so gave a brief description of my friend Elijah Chaila. 'That's him,' she confirmed. I was able to tell her that he was indeed a Christian and that he had just recently joined our church. Isn't it wonderful when grace radiates from a heart that God has made kind?

Growing up, we had a family friend we called Uncle George (although he wasn't really our uncle). Uncle George was a godly Methodist minister. He had served for a time as a missionary in Sri Lanka. The Christian author, Ajith Fernando, refers to George as 'the pastor of my teenage years, who influenced me in the beauty of godliness.'[5] Just observing gentle godly people like Uncle George increases our confidence in the goodness of God. Why not aim at being the sort of gracious and kind person that is good for the mental health of others?

LOOK AFTER YOURSELF

One time, after giving a talk at a church outreach event in West Cork, I was talking to a number of people when it was pointed out that I had mentioned nothing about the struggles of living with someone who has depression or anxiety.

So, I have asked a friend to tell of her experience of living in a family where more than one person has struggled with anxiety and depression. She mentioned sadness, loneliness and a lack of emotional nourishment when people feel unable to engage with you. Joy, laughter and hope can be in short supply. She spoke of the importance to her of knowing the love of God, the support of an amazing sibling and a couple of good Christian friends.

As with any illness, life will be disrupted. Your depressed or anxious loved one may not be able to enjoy

---

5. Ajith Fernando, *Leadership Lifestyle* (Mumbai: Gospel Literature Service, 1985), p. 12.

doing the things you do together. They may have less energy. They may be irritable. They may be less enjoyable company. It's okay to admit that this is difficult. If you are committed to working through these difficulties together, you may actually find that in the long term your relationship is strengthened.

Look after your own well-being. You may need the support of friends to talk through how you are coping with your loved one's illness. You may want to talk to others about anything but the illness. Take time out. Don't feel guilty about still doing things that you enjoy. There will be times when you say the wrong thing or lose your patience; accept God's forgiveness when that happens and don't beat yourself up. Do not let the crisis cause you to neglect your spiritual life but try to lean heavily on the love of your Heavenly Father.

CONCLUSION: HE COMFORTS US IN OUR PAIN SO THAT WE CAN COMFORT OTHERS

Ed Stetzer claims from his research, that, 'in many ways, the church, the supposed haven for sufferers, is not a safe place for those who struggle with mental illness.'[6] It is a tragedy when people are afraid to be vulnerable because of what critics and gossips will say. It is an outright denial of the gospel of grace when people in the church need to pretend that they are strong and sorted. We live in a fallen world where all of us are broken, and all of us have weaknesses. Churches need to be open about mental health issues and work to remove the stigma of this normal abnormality.

---

6. Ed Stetzer, 'The Christian Struggle with Mental Illness', (www.christianitytoday.com, May 23, 2016).

While some churches can be less than helpful to those who are going through struggles with their mental health this has not been my personal experience. The two churches that I have pastored as I worked through these issues publicly could not have been kinder. In truth, like any community of people, there will be people who are helpful and those who are not. I think that the help offered by those who really care outweighs the frustration that may be caused by those who say insensitive things.

I remember going down to the kitchen in the church hall, having told the congregation I wouldn't be visiting them for the next two months. There was one of my friends in a flood of tears. She felt so much empathy for me. It was deeply touching. I could have no doubts about her love. In that church many people were open about their mental health issues. In fact, I used to joke that depression was one of the defining features of that church. I am convinced it was not because we had more mental health problems than other churches, but because people felt safe to be real with each other.

When I experienced my more recent breakdown and subsequent depression, Doctor Elijah offered support and medical advice. Another friend who had been a psychiatric nurse took me for coffee when I had the strength and gave me some very useful insights. I regularly received WhatsApp messages from another to say that she was praying, and I knew she would back those words with action. The whole atmosphere of the church was one of love and kindness.

If you are loving someone who is depressed and anxious, there will be times when it will be a struggle. Their progress may be slow. There may be times when you are tired of hearing about how they feel. You may be frustrated at not knowing what to say. They may always be looking for reassurance. But draw on the compassion of 'the God and Father of our Lord Jesus Christ, the Father of compassion, the God of all comfort, who comforts us in all our troubles, so that we can comfort those in any trouble with the comfort we ourselves receive from God' (2 Cor. 1:3-4).

We live in a fallen world where Christians often suffer with depression and anxiety. We have a Heavenly Father who has accepted us by His grace and we are blessed to live in a spiritual family where we are commanded to share each other's burdens. We draw on the compassion of Christ to have the strength to do so.

Let's pray to the God of all comfort:

Gentle and mighty Jesus, a bruised reed You will not break and a smouldering candle You will not snuff out. You are unparalleled in compassion. You cared for the crowds even when You were exhausted. Help me to care for my bruised and broken loved one. Let me be patient and gentle. Help me listen and concentrate. Help me speak words that are truly encouraging. Show me what I can do for them. May I speak as one broken person with another. May I model the grace that You have shown to me. Amen.

Conclusion:

You are not alone

In August 2001 I had a bit of a meltdown. I was extremely anxious with my fears of being beyond grace and struggling with dark intrusive thoughts. I rang my friend Peter, who has always been a rock to me. He was in London working at the time. He suggested that I come over and spend some time with him. I flew over a few weeks later on September 11th.

One of the days I went into the heart of London. On the way into the centre, I said to God, 'Lord, I would love to see All Souls, Langham Place' (a church whose teaching has helped me), 'and I would love to see my friend June' (a dear friend who was living in London and who I had not seen for a long time). 'But I am not going to ask you for these because I could have looked up a map and I could have got June's number before I travelled. I'm just saying what I would love.'

I had no idea how big London was and as I wandered, none of the churches I looked at was All Souls. Then I came to Oxford Circus and went into a record shop. There on a CD cover I saw the name of a song called 'Antichrist' and

I started to struggle with obsessive thoughts about evil. I quickly left the shop and hurried up the street, mumbling to myself to keep the thoughts out of my head. I was going to get on the next Tube and head back to Peter's flat. At the top of the street was a church. It was the last church I would see before leaving the city centre. It was All Souls. I had looked at so many churches and in the end stumbled across the one I was looking for.

When I got on the Tube, I had a change or two to get to Peter's. There, as I waited for the Tube, I glanced to my left and there was June, just five metres away. What a 'coincidence'! Among the thousands of church buildings and millions of people, I had stumbled across the two I had told God I had most hoped to see. It happened at a time when I was in great distress. It seems that God wanted to reassure me of His love. It was a wonderful kindness.

That in itself raises questions. Why doesn't God always intervene like that? During my last deep depression there were times I doubted God's very existence. There are times when we suffer, and yet God feels absent. As I write I have the words of a friend in my head, who told Caroline how hard she is finding it to trust God's faithfulness as she watches someone she loves suffer terrible pain. The truth is that God is with us in the darkness as well as the light. For reasons that we can't understand He sometimes calms the storm and at other times He lets us pass through the storm. Sometimes we know that we are held in His hand and at other times it feels that we are all alone. I pray that God will help you know that God is close to the brokenhearted and saves those who are crushed in spirit (Ps. 34:18).

We have seen that sickness and brokenness are part of living in a fallen world. Struggles with mental health are just like any other health issues. There can be a variety of contributing factors, so it is important to seek a variety of help. Faith in the good news of grace should help your emotional well-being. But Christians live a life where joy is mingled with sorrow. It is good to talk. Keep on listening and talking to God. Talk to your doctor. Don't feel that it is unspiritual to take medication where appropriate. Seek to grow in your confidence in the character of God. Remember that God is a good Father who wants you to be secure in His love.

I want to finish this book with three thoughts: you are not alone, try not to lose hope and seek to honour God in the darkness.

YOU ARE NOT ALONE

I was once asked to speak at a Faith Mission event that was being held at a rural church. There were a reasonable number there, given that it was a midweek night. Most of the people were of retirement age. I suspected that they were just looking for an evening of company and that the topic of my struggles with OCD was only of mild interest to them. I was wrong. After the service I hung around waiting to see if anyone wanted to talk with me about what I had said. Initially just one person, who struggled terribly with depression, approached me. But as I moved into the hall for a cuppa, I was surprised to find that lots of people wanted to talk. One man told me about his daughter who had died by suicide, and a friend I had not seen in years shared with me his struggles with obsessive thoughts similar to mine. People talked about themselves and those they cared for. I was taken aback by how much this topic touches a raw nerve in so many.

Something similar happened some months later. I was doing much the same talk to a larger group of people. I offered to pray with anyone who wanted after the service. I prayed with a steady trickle of people for about an hour. Again, people shared their own struggles and their concern for those they loved. In truth we all know people who are suffering from anxiety and depression.

If you suffer with anxiety and/or depression you are not alone. You are surrounded by people who are experiencing their own pain. You are also not alone as a Christian who struggles with anxiety and depression. Plenty of godly people who know emotional pain are in the pages of Scripture, in the history of the church and in your own congregation.

TRY NOT TO LOSE HOPE

My last bout of depression and anxiety was different from anything I had suffered before. As a result, I feared that it might not lift. I thought that the rest of my life might be lived in the pits. The psychiatrist I saw at that time did not share this worry. She said that it would lift, and it did. She explained that the feelings of depression would be at their worst when I woke in the morning and would improve during the day. That is helpful to know. The day will get better. For me, however, I began to so dread what was to come when I woke, knowing how wretched I would feel first thing in the morning that I didn't want to go to sleep at night.

During that time of depression, I was struck by how important a sense of hope is. When you are in the middle of a crisis, you need to remind yourself that this too will pass. A friend told me how she could not help her sister gain any hope when she was depressed. I would urge you to do everything not to give up hope, and to remind yourself that you have not always been in these depths and you will not always be in these depths.

SEEK TO HONOUR GOD IN THE DARKNESS

Finally, I remember when I was in a place of deep darkness walking around a city centre park trying desperately to connect with God. I started singing, 'Jesus, be the centre'. I wish I had done such things more often at that time. I think that at that moment my faith was as dependent on God as it had ever been. Our faith can be wonderfully alive even when our heart feels broken, and our feelings seem dead. This is a thought picked up by Bible translator, J. B. Phillips, who wrote in a letter to a friend: 'These periods of spiritual dryness which every saint has known are the very times when your need of God is greatest. To worship Him may or may not bring back the lost "feeling", but your contact with God in prayer and praise will strengthen you spiritually whether you feel it or not ... Times of spiritual apathy are the very times when we can do most to prove our love for God, and I have no doubt we bring most joy to His heart when we defy our feelings and act in spite of them.'[1]

May God give us strength to know His love and live for His glory in all the pains and stress of life as we live in this fallen world. May we remember that He sent His one and only Son to take the punishment of our guilt that we might became His dearly loved children. May we have a deep awareness that He is our Heavenly

---

1. Quoted in Doctor Gaius Davies, *Genius and Grace* (London: Hodder and Stoughton, 1992), p. 228.

Father, even when He seems absent. May we have confidence in His character, even when His ways are a mystery to us.

Let's pray:

> I do love You Lord, although I know that my love for You is shallow. I know that You are here for me, although it can seem to me like You are absent. You will deliver me! You are the only one I can turn to for help. You are the only one who truly understands me. I cry to You when I need help, and You do listen to me. Even when everything falls apart, I somehow know that You are there. You are helping me. I know that You will deliver me. You are my rock. You have accepted me as Your child. You are with me in my troubles. You will bring me through my pain. Amen.
>
> (Adapted from Psalm 18)

Selected bibliography and recommended reading

Bunyan, John. *Grace Abounding to the Chief of Sinners.* (Wisconsin: Aneko Press, 2018). This is really a record of how Bunyan came to have an assurance of his salvation. It's short and it has useful insights.

Cipollone, Chris. *Down Not Out.* (Surrey: The Good Book Company, 2018). This book is a short, helpful and readable theological reflection on depression and anxiety born out of the author's own struggles.

Collins, Sarah and Haynes, Jayne. *Dealing with Depression.* (Ross-Shire, Scotland: Christian Focus Publications, 2011). This is a short readable book that deals with causes and helps for the depressed Christian.

Elshout, Arie. *Overcoming Spiritual Depression.* (Grand Rapids, Michigan: Reformation Heritage Books, 2006). This is a short look at the life and depression of Elijah.

Eswine, Zack. *Spurgeon's Sorrow*. (Ross-Shire, Scotland: Christian Focus Publications, 2014). I find the great preacher Spurgeon to be a fascinating character. Spurgeon suffered with terrible depression, and Eswine's short book provides fascinating insights.

Greene-McCreight, Kathryn. *Darkness Is My Only Companion*. (Grand Rapids, Michigan: Brazos Press, 2006). In this book Kathryn talks about her very deep depression. She gives a very moving account of the lead-up to her hospitalisation. In this she gives good advice concerning the issues that this raises for the immediate family of those suffering. The second part of the book concerns her theological reflections on mental health. I found myself less engaged in this second part because she was coming from a more sacramental understanding of the Christian faith than me.

Hastings, Sharon. *Wrestling With My Thoughts*. (London: Inter-Varsity Press, 2020). I found this to be one of the most open, raw and engaging books that I have ever read. Sharon shares her experiences of severe depression and anxiety. It is a great book for those with mental health issues to relate to, although it is also a great book for those seeking to understand those who suffer. It finishes with a very helpful question and answer section.

Lloyd-Jones, Martyn. *Spiritual Depression*. (London: Marshall Pickering, 1965). I am not sure that the title 'Spiritual Depression' is all that helpful for this book. It doesn't deal with the medical issues around depression and anxiety. I thought that it might be better called

'Living in Grace'. This is a reasonably heavy read. It shapes your outlook on how the gospel should affect our thinking, particularly in areas where misunderstanding the gospel may make us feel despondent. You can read about Lloyd-Jones' views on the medical treatment of depression in his book, *Healing and The Scriptures,* which I accessed online.

Meynell, Mark. *When Darkness Seems My Closest Friend.* (London: Inter-Varsity Press, 2017). This is an extraordinary book written by a fellow 'cave-dweller'. It is finely written blending Mark's own story with his thoughts on poetry, books and music.

Murray, David. *Christians Get Depressed Too.* (Grand Rapids, Michigan: Reformation Heritage Books, 2010). I first heard David and Shona Murray on a podcast that Caroline encouraged me to listen to when I was depressed. I found their story and advice compelling. This book is another short and useful look at the causes and cures for depression. He is seeking to deal with the super-spiritual denials that real Christians shouldn't get depressed. He looks at the complexity, causes and cures for depression. He also has advice for caregivers. David wrote a book called *Reset* (Crossway, 2017), and another with Shona called *ReFresh* (Crossway, 2017). These books are designed to give helpful life tips to prevent burnout. I didn't realise that the book with Shona was aimed for women, but it did me no harm.

Murray, David. *The Happy Christian.* (Nashville, Tennessee: Nelson Books, 2015). The subtitle of this book reads, 'Ten Ways to Be a Joyful Believer in a Gloomy World.' I thought this subtitle made it sound like the sort of shallow self-help book that you would be fobbed off with on religious television. This is anything but a shallow book. Murray is a sound and thoughtful Christian who writes in an engaging style. The book is filled with practical Bible-shaped wisdom. It is a great help in thinking through how your outlook affects your mood.

Thomas, Alan. *Tackling Mental Health Together.* (London: Inter-Varsity Press, 2017). A well-written and informative book written by a psychiatrist seeking to help church leaders care for those with mental health problems.

Welch, Edward T. *Depression: Looking Up from the Stubborn Darkness.* (Greensboro: New Growth Press, 2011). I found this one of the best helps in coming to understand the causes of depression. It is a thorough and readable book.

Whitney, Donald S. *How Can I Be Sure I'm a Christian?* (Carol Stream, Illinois: NavPress, 1994). There are many good books on the topic of assurance of your salvation. Be careful not to become obsessed with simply seeking reassurance from such reading. It might be time to stop reading, addressing underlying insecurities, and praying that God would enable you to see that you really are one of His children.

Williams, Chris et. al. *I Am Not Supposed to Feel This Way.* (London: Hodder and Stoughton, 2002). This is a thorough self-help approach to depression and anxiety. It is full of useful material and has an element of workbook to it. Our church bought a number of copies of this book to share. It covers all the bases. It also includes advice for how the church and pastors can help the depressed and anxious.

Acknowledgments

Thanks to Jackie O'Regan, who reads my blog and told me I should write a book. Thanks to those who gave theological, medical, psychological, grammatical and personal insights: Peter Orr, John Alderdice, Lewis Porter, Michaela Tuccilo, Brenda O'Connell, Elijah Chaila, John Samuel, Peter Kearns, Angela Mellett, Tim Lewis, Caroline Ritchie, Alice Marshall, Luisa Richardson, Ieteke Oggle, Peter Grier, Eoin O'Doherty, Wyn Bryans, Patrick Mitchel, David Blevins, Mark Ellis, Elaine Johnston, Sheila Begg, and Jack and Claire Solomon. So many people read drafts of this book that I am not sure there will be anyone left to buy the book. I love my family at Limerick Baptist, and am so privileged to share the eldership with Edwin Tutty and John Ryan. Thanks too for the kindness of Christian Focus Publications for publishing the book. In particular the kindness of Donnie Morrison, the guidance of Rosanna Burton and Irene Roberts and the brilliant editorial eye of Helen Jones. I really am grateful.

I must mention my parents who are such a wonderful support. This book is dedicated to my wife Caroline – you are at your best when God calls on you to exercise your great empathy and practical wisdom.

TRACK
CHRISTIAN
LIFE

JOHN C.
KWASNY

SERIES EDITED BY
JOHN PERRITT

A STUDENT'S GUIDE TO
DEPRESSION

Track: Depression

A Student's Guide to Depression

John C. Kwasny

- Grounds depression in a biblical worldview
- Written by biblical counsellor
- For students and young adults

Biblical counsellor John Kwasny helpfully tackles the issue of depression in this latest addition to the popular Track series. He addresses the ways depression can affect us, and gives helpful biblical advice on how we should react. This short book will be helpful for students and young adults as they encounter depression themselves, or as they seek to support friends or family members.

ISBN: 978-1-5271-0797-7

Christian Focus Publications

Our mission statement —

STAYING FAITHFUL

In dependence upon God we seek to impact the world through literature faithful to His infallible Word, the Bible. Our aim is to ensure that the Lord Jesus Christ is presented as the only hope to obtain forgiveness of sin, live a useful life and look forward to heaven with Him.

Our books are published in four imprints:

CHRISTIAN FOCUS

Popular works including biographies, commentaries, basic doctrine and Christian living.

CHRISTIAN HERITAGE

Books representing some of the best material from the rich heritage of the church.

MENTOR

Books written at a level suitable for Bible College and seminary students, pastors, and other serious readers. The imprint includes commentaries, doctrinal studies, examination of current issues and church history.

CF4•K

Children's books for quality Bible teaching and for all age groups: Sunday school curriculum, puzzle and activity books; personal and family devotional titles, biographies and inspirational stories — because you are never too young to know Jesus!

Christian Focus Publications Ltd,
Geanies House, Fearn, Ross-shire,
IV20 1TW, Scotland, United Kingdom.
www.christianfocus.com
blog.christianfocus.com